Grandpa's Big Book on Money

Grandpa's Big Book on Money

Vincent Bath

Illustrated By Adam "Bear" Brown

IC
PRESS

Idea Creations Press

Published in the United States by Idea Creations Press LLC.

Library of Congress Control Number: 2025920123
ISBN 978-1948804370

This book is written by Vincent Bath, it is neither made, provided, approved nor endorsed by Intellectual Reserve, Inc. or The Church of Jesus Christ of Latter-day Saints. Any content or opinions expressed, implied or included in are solely those of Vincent Bath and not those of Intellectual Reserve, Inc. or The Church of Jesus Christ of Latter-day Saints.

www.ideacreationspress.com

Contents

I dedicate this book to my wonderful wife (and your grandmother) Debra. She gave me purpose, love, six wonderful children (your parents) and stuck with me through thick and thin while I learned the business of life. Thank you my dear.

Why is Grandpa Writing this Book?

Over the almost seven decades that I've lived, I've learned a lot about personal finance. It's come by listening to and watching smart people, observing a lot of dumb people, enjoying my own successes and making lots of mistakes. I've also been watched over and blessed by a merciful God, who has bailed me out more times than I can count.

Having wisdom at my age is a good thing, but I've often wished I'd known all of this stuff when I was young – say eleven. Actually, I would have settled for it at 21, or 31, or even 41 – early enough to have shared it with my children. **The bad news** is that it came too late for them. **The good news** is that it's come in time for my grandchildren – to whom this book is written.

I've thought about writing this book for about 25 years. **The bad news** is that life lessons from the School of Hard Knocks got it the way. **The good news** is that I know so much more now than I did 25 years ago. For one thing, I've read some very helpful books on personal finance that I highly recommend including, *The Millionaire Next Door* (Stanley and Danko, 1998); *Rich Dad, Poor Dad* (Kiyosaki and Letcher, 1997); and *The Total Money Makeover* (Ramsey, 2003). So now, five years into retirement, I'm ready to start sharing what I know.

As I start, I want to make it very clear that I have not always done everything right. It's taken me a long time to gain the knowledge I'm about to share and even when I **did** know better, I guess I was determined to pay the stupid tax.

You, my grandchildren, will also make your share of mistakes. It's an inevitable part of the process, but if my parents or my grandparents had gained the wisdom I now have and had shared it with me, **and** if I had listened **and** applied it, I would have had greater power, over decades, to help, bless and lift my family and others.

Power is the real gift I am giving you here!

Because I want this book to be helpful, I'll give you a "heads up" about how it's put together and how it's intended to be used. It's divided into the following three parts.

- Chapters 1-4 are the **WHY** chapters. They include a brief overview of my philosophy of money and why good money management is important. It's written on about an 8th grade level and could easily be read in one setting, but I suggest you take it a bite at a time, think about each principal and, hopefully, buy in.

- Then there is a short section entitled ***Tots to Teens: Milestones in Financial Independence*** in which I chart a path to financial independence broken down by age. The purpose behind this section is to give you a framework and some mile posts to guide your financial journey. I have included quite a bit of white space on this chart so that you can make notes for planning and tracking your efforts.

- Chapters 5-8 are the **HOW** chapters. In these chapters I attempt to expand on the WHYs and give you the benefit of my experience. I tried to write in 8th grade language, but used terms and concepts that are more advanced. To help you understand, I've included lots definitions and explanations in text boxes throughout these chapters. There's A LOT of information in these chapters, so much so that I've actually divided some of the chapters into subsections. It is A LOT, but if you can **understand** the principles in these chapters, you'll have a great start in becoming financially independent. If you can **master** them, you'll actually be master of your money.

I suggest that you read the WHY chapters **early**. If you can't yet read (or read well), have your parents read and explain them to you. You should read them **often** so that you can understand and internalize the principles. Before you can implement the HOWs, you will need to understand the WHYs and before you can really do the hard work of the HOWs, you'll need to buy into the WHYs.

Tots to Teens is designed to be used in conjunction with the HOW chapters. I imagine you bouncing back and forth between the two sections as you learn new things. It's designed to give you an insider map to the journey and motivate you, not make you feel like a slacker or depress you. If you are behind "schedule", start where you are and do the best you can.

The HOW chapters are the **big kid** part of the book. I do not expect you to read this part unless and until you are ready. And you will be ready when you are curious enough, or sick and tired enough, or want to get started badly enough.

I've tried to imagine us actually talking and learning together as I've written this book. As I anticipated questions, comments and confusions, I wrote them into the text. Whenever you see dialogue written in *red-italic-bold*, that is me voicing your part in the discussion.

Finally, Grandpa has put some stuff in the back of the book. Because I will always have more to say about a subject than there is room for, I have included a couple of appendices that you may read if you want to know more, and more, and more and... Also, being a member of the Church of Jesus Christ of Latter-day Saints, Grandpa speaks (and has written in) fluent Mormonese. So, he has included a glossary in the back to define some of the LDS-centric terms he uses.

Like I said, this is my gift to you. Please let it bless your life.

Chapter 1: What Are the Governing Principals of this Book?

Here are some basic undergirding principles I want you to understand and apply. If you can do that, everything else will just to fall into place.

1. **Money is just a tool**

Money is neither good nor bad. It is just a tool. It is what we **do for and with money and how we feel about money** that makes it good or bad.

Money is a medium of exchange. If I want something from someone, I can give them money and they will give me what I want. If someone wants me to work for them, they can agree to pay me in money. Money makes the transactions of business, trade and labor easier because almost everybody understands the value of money.

Money has taken many forms over the years. Long ago, people used shells, beads, gems, cattle, or any other number of things they believed to be valuable. When people decided that gold and silver were valuable, they started to make those metals into coins; it was easier than herding around your cattle all day. Later they printed paper money or wrote checks, which had no other value than a promise to pay the holder gold or silver; it was easier than carrying around those heavy and bulky coins.

Over the years our money has become less and less tangible. Today we use a lot less paper money and coins. Most of our financial transactions are electronic and no tangible assets trade hands at all. We all just agree that our employer's electronic transfer to our bank account is of value. And the store owners agree that swiping our debit card transfers part of that value to their bank accounts. It's all based on a mutual agreement as to the value of those electronic transfers as "money".

Money is good when it is used to buy good things and do good things and **money is bad** when it is used to buy bad things and do bad things, but that's not the whole story. The bad side of money includes the unhealthy and unproductive things we can think and feel about it. It's bad to obsess about money. It's bad to do unrighteous things to get money. It's bad to think that money can save us.

God commanded, "Thou shalt have no other gods before Me!" (Exodus 20:3 KJV) Whatever we give our time, effort, resources and devotion to, **or** whatever we think has the power to save us, can become a god to us. Strategizing, working hard or being dedicated to getting money becomes bad when they take the place of the other important things in your life, especially your family and duty to God.

Through Isaiah God taught, "I, *even* I, *am* the L ORD; and beside me *there is* no saviour." (Isaiah 43:11KJV) Money can be a powerful tool and sometimes it can "save" us from temporal troubles, but it did not create the world; design the Plan of Happiness; provide us with bodies, a wonderful earthly existence, or a Savior. It cannot forgive your sins; heal your heart; understand and succor you; resurrect, justify or exalt you. Only God can do these things and only God deserves our worship.

In *The Book of Mormon*, Jacob talked to some of the Nephites who had crossed the line and were worshipping riches. He told them how to sort out their priorities when it came to money:

> But before ye seek for riches, seek ye for the kingdom of God.
> And after ye have obtained a hope in Christ ye shall obtain riches, if ye
> seek them; and ye will seek them for the intent to do good—to clothe the
> naked, and to feed the hungry, and to liberate the captive, and administer
> relief to the sick and the afflicted. (Jacob 2:18-19)

Jacob uses the term "riches" in his counsel, and this is a good point on which to end our discussion of this first principle. When we say "riches", we often think "money", but we sometimes don't understand how "rich" we are in things other than money. Let me give you just one example.

All of my grandchildren currently live in the United States of America and because of that they enjoy almost unlimited economic potential. They can all receive a quality education, own personal property, start businesses, join labor unions, move freely around the country, and invest in financial markets. And all of these wonderful privileges are protected by America's society and laws. This potential is very much a form of wealth. It is riches. It is a tool. And the rules of conduct and attitude apply to this tool, just as they do to money. It should be used for good and kept in proper perspective.

But wait, there's more!

This "pursuit of happiness" outlined in the Declaration of Independence is a God-given, inalienable right, but that right was not realized without a price. It cost blood. It cost sweat. It cost tears. And we, today, stand on the shoulders of those giants who bled, who perspired and who cried. We need to treat their sacrifice with respect and be thankful. We need to use this purchased potential wisely, deny it to none, and share it freely with all.

2. Everything belongs to God

Now that we have established the proper attitudes we need to have about money (and riches) we, ironically, turn to the second principle, which is that none of it belongs to us anyway. Numerous scriptures teach that God created the universe and everything in it and that it is all His.

> I, the Lord, stretched out the heavens, and built the earth, my
> very handiwork; and all things therein are mine. (D&C 104:14)

"All things" includes the earth and all its mineral resources (including the soil we use to grow our food); the atmosphere and all of the gases (including the very air we breathe); all of the machinery and processes (including respiration and photosynthesis); and the intellectual property (including the intelligent design He used to create it all). This is just a partial list of the things God owns, but it makes the point. It is all His!

What a merciful God! He provides all this for our use and enjoyment. We should be very, very grateful. However, all that God has given us is more than a loan and even more than a gift. **It is a stewardship!**

A steward is someone who cares for and manages the property of his master. His stewardship is not just **the things** for which he is asked to care, but **the responsibility, the trust and the authority** to do the job. Periodically, the steward must make a report to the master and his work is evaluated. If he does well, he is promoted. If he does poorly, he gets demoted or fired.

Grandpa's favorite resource for learning about stewardship is found in Jesus' parable of the talents. It was one of the last things Jesus taught the very disciples that would oversee His earthly kingdom. He was preparing them to be His stewards. Take a minute to read Matthew 25:14-30.

I'll wait!

The parable is pretty straight forward, but there is one part that is often misunderstood. Most people think that the master is angry with the last steward because the steward didn't make any money. He's not! He's angry because the steward didn't even try. The master basically said, "All I asked was that you do your best. You could at least have put it in a savings account and collected some interest!"

God put it this way in our dispensation.

> For the power is in them, wherein they are agents unto themselves. And inasmuch as men do good they shall in nowise lose their reward.
> But he that doeth not anything until he is commanded, and receiveth a commandment with doubtful heart, and keepeth it with slothfulness, the same is damned. (D&C 58:28-29)

So, now that you understand the basics of stewardship let's apply it to money. All money and riches (along with the talents, abilities and opportunities used to get them) belong to God. He has allotted to each of us a portion of those resources according to His infinite wisdom.

You've been evaluated by God, been found willing and able, allotted resources, and charged to be good stewards over them. Your job is to make the best out of what you have been given and return it all to God. You're among the most blessed people on the face of the earth and in all of history. Don't bury, misuse or squander what you have been given. Your stewardship interviews (and there will be many) will focus on your efforts to do your best with what you have been given, how you conducted yourself in the management of what you have been given, and how you returned it all to God.

3. You are the captain of your own cruise.

I want you to imagine that Grandpa and Grandma took all our teenage grandchildren on a cruise to the Caribbean. It could be really fun to sail, eat and recreate together. We would all be on the same boat, but would we all have the same experience?

What if one of you got seasick, didn't bring any Dramamine and spent the week throwing up in your cabin?

What if one of you didn't wear any sunscreen, stayed out in the sun the whole first day and spent the rest of the week nursing a sunburn in your cabin?

What if one of you ate something to which you were allergic, swelled up like a pufferfish and were too embarrassed to go out in public until the swelling went down.

What if you misunderstood and packed for an Alaskan cruise instead?

What if… **okay that's enough to make the point.**

So, whose responsibility was it to make sure you had Dramamine, wore sunscreen, knew what foods to avoid and packed the right clothes? Grandma and Grandpa? Your parents? Your cousins? The captain? The cruise director? No! Expecting any of these people to be responsible for you is childish.

And so, it is with money!

You are the captain of your own financial cruise and it doesn't matter if you are sailing on a luxury liner or rowing a leaky dingy, you are in charge. You need to take that responsibility seriously – all the time. Grandpa will teach you some important concepts in this book, but it's up to you to learn and apply them.

I cannot overemphasize this point. If you are financially secure and successful it will be your fault. If you lose money, get ripped off or find yourself in financial trouble it will be your fault!

4. There is a right way to climb a ladder

Ladders are very helpful tools, allowing you to reach and work in places you could not otherwise, but if you use a ladder improperly, you can get seriously injured or killed. Following a few simple safety rules can help you use a ladder safely and effectively.

There are financial ladders that work similarly to physical ladders. Climbing such ladders can help you reach financial heights and achieve financial goals, but misusing a financial ladder can be monetarily and emotional dangerous. Here are three simple rules that can help you use your financial ladders safely and effectively.

You need to choose the right ladder for the job. A 24-foot extension ladder works well for cleaning out the rain gutters, but would be a poor tool for changing a light bulb in the ceiling fan. Use the right ladder for the job. And the same goes for financial ladders.

Education is a great example of a financial ladder. A good education will help you work smarter and make more money. **But** all educations are not created equal. For example, a bachelor's degree in *Education* will get you an annual starting salary of about $34,900, while a bachelor's degree in *Chemical Engineering* will get you an annual starting salary of about $63,000. Both of these degrees cost about the same to obtain, but pay vastly different returns on that investment.

Grandpa is not saying you have to be a chemical engineer, especially if you don't like chemistry. What I am saying is that different educational ladders will allow you to climb to different places and you need to make sure you are buying (with your tuition and effort) the right ladder – one that will take you where you want to go.

While a ladder can help you get a leg up (pun totally intended), you must make sure your ladder is set up on stable and level ground before you start climbing it. It's the same with financial ladders.

Leverage (sometimes called "using other people's money") is a great financial ladder. It can allow you to get a greater return on your investments and invest in ways you couldn't otherwise. For example, how many people do you know that could save up enough money to pay cash for their first home? Not many, I predict. Most people leverage what they **have** saved by obtaining a mortgage that pays 80% or more of the price of the home. They pay it back (with interest) over 30 years, while enjoying the advantages of owning the home. This plan is a reasonable option and an effective ladder to climb. **But** if you borrow for a home on top of other significant debts, *or* buy before your income is stable, **or** buy a more expensive home than you need, you're setting your ladder up on shaky ground and it won't take too much of a financial crisis (job loss, major medical expenses) to tip your ladder over. You could lose your home and your investment and ruin your credit rating.

Climb your ladder the right way. The safe way to climb a physical ladder is to take it one rung at a time, keeping three points of contact (two feet and a hand or two hands and a foot) at all times. Properly climbing financial ladders involves similar principles.

Take for example, the financial ladder called investment. Financial investment is when you put your resources into a venture with the hope of making a profit. Solid, legitimate investment ladders exist and can be very helpful in your financial life. **But**, believe it or not, some people try to climb investment ladders by jumping two or three rungs or by reaching too far from the ladder to get something they want. A classic example of this is trying to get rich quick – usually by being suckered into get-rich-quick schemes.

Some of these schemes, like buying lottery tickets, are obvious. Others are not so obvious. You may be asked to invest in a stock, business or product with promises of outrageous returns. You may be offered a very good paying job or business opportunity, but are asked to put money upfront to "buy-in" or get training and supplies. You may be invited to join a multi-level marketing business where the focus of the business is to recruit people into your sales team rather than actually selling a product or service. All of these scams thrive on greed and impatience and almost always end badly. You can do well and even get rich by using the investment ladder. But you must invest your money, time, effort, and reputation patiently and wisely – step by step and with a good footing on and grasp of sound and time-tested investing principles.

5. There is power in self-reliance and provident living

At some points in life, everyone needs help. It is part of God's plan. When you need help, seek it, take it and be grateful for it. When you are in a position to give help, do it freely and humbly. Heavenly Father is pleased when we both seek and give help, but He wants this help offered in His "own way" (see D&C

104:14-16).

That way is for each of us to become self-reliant so that we can stand in a position to serve and care for others, so they can become self-reliant and be in a position to serve and care for others, so they can become self-reliant so that they can .... **You get the point!** Church leaders define self-reliance as "the ability, commitment, and effort to provide the

> *It is important to mention that self-reliance applies to all aspects of our lives, not just finances. And it is important that you work on being self-reliant and then helping others in all aspects of life, but for the purposes of this book we will be talking about financial self-reliance.*

spiritual and temporal necessities of life for ourselves and families." (*Handbook 2: Administering the Church* (2010), 6.1.1) Once you can care for yourself and your family, you can be in a position to help others.

Financial self-reliance is achieved through provident living. Elder Robert D. Hales defined provident living as "*joyfully* living within our means, being *content* with what we have, avoiding excessive debt, and *diligently* saving and preparing for rainy-day emergencies. [Emphasis added]" (*Becoming Provident Providers Temporally and Spiritually*, April 2009 General Conference). His definition is filled with one-word power statements. Re-read it, focusing on the words I have italicized and bolded.

I'll wait!

Provident living is not just the way poor, miserly or obsessive people live. It is the pattern that God has given us to become self-reliant, strong and confident (especially in our finances). This book will return to this theme often and, if you are wise, this theme will be woven into the tapestry of your life.

The Doctrine and Covenants helps us catch the scope and power of this principle.

> Behold, this is the preparation wherewith I prepare you, and the foundation, and the ensample which I give unto you, whereby you may accomplish the commandments which are given you;
>
> That through my providence, notwithstanding the tribulation which shall descend upon you, that the church may **stand independent above all other creatures** beneath the celestial world; [Emphasis Added] (D&C 78:13-14)

Can you recognize the power in self-reliance, the ability to stand independent above all other creatures and to be able to choose who you will be and what you will do and to reach out your hand and lift others to that same independence?

The pathway to this power is through provident living and often requires help to get started. To be strong enough and generous enough and humble enough to give help is divine behavior, but it is also divine behavior to be strong and humble enough to seek, take and be grateful for help to get started.

Chapter 2: What is Your Plan?

As captain of your cruise, you would be foolish to try to take life's financial journey without navigation tools and the navigation tool you need for a successful journey is a financial plan. Not just any plan, but a well-designed plan. And it's not enough to have a well-designed plan, it must be well executed. In this chapter we will talk about planning and execution in general. Then, in another section, Grandpa will get more specific about the logistics of financial plans and execution.

The first step in designing a plan is deciding what you want. What is your **WHY**? Understanding what you want not only makes planning simpler, it will motivate you to follow through when the going gets tough.

A **purpose** is a well thought out and clear statement of what you want. Anything less is just a wish or whim. While a purpose is powerful and motivating, a wish or whim is generally common and weak. As Great-Grandma Bath used to say: "If wishes were fishes, we'd all have a fry."

The late billionaire and philanthropist John Huntsman Sr. grew up poor and, of course, wished he could be rich, but the real reason he was so motivated to be wealthy was because he wanted to cure cancer. This is partly because his mother died from cancer as he held her in his arms. After he became rich, he established and was a driving force behind the Huntsman Cancer Center at the University of Utah and donated hundreds of millions of dollars to fund it. **That is the difference between a wish and a purpose!** Your purpose may not be that impressive in dollars, but it can be as powerful and grand in terms of what is important to you. Knowing your WHY will make a huge difference in the design and execution of your plan.

If you are reading this at age eleven, you may not have the understanding to determine your grand purpose. Your purpose may just be to buy a nice Christmas gift for your mother. But, even at a young age, you can start learning this process.

If you are reading this at 16, your ability to determine serious and motivating WHYS is much greater and you definitely need to start thinking about this stuff. At the very least, you should be considering a career choice and thinking about a mission or your post-secondary education.

By the time you are a young adult, you need to get serious about finding your purpose. It will require some study, thought, prayer, and talking with people you respect and trust. Your purpose may get tweaked over the years as you gain experience and wisdom, but do not put it off.

Once you have determined your WHY, it will be time to plan out your HOW – a SMART plan to make it happen. A smart plan is made up of a set of well-thought-out SMART goals that cascade down from and support your purpose. If you have no idea what I just wrote, don't worry, we'll go over it step by step in another section. Just remember, for now, that goal setting and plan design are very basic skills and can be used to improve all aspects of your life. The more you practice them, the better you will get at it.

When you've made your plan, it's time to go to work and make it happen. This is called **execution** and a plan is only as good as its execution. Every year people make New Year's Resolutions and give up on them in a few weeks, days or even hours. Here are a couple of tips to keep this from happening to you.

How do you eat an elephant? One bite at a time. Whatever your purpose, break it down into top, and then mid, and then low-level goals, each level getting more specific and having a smaller and smaller task to accomplish. (Again, we will talk about how to do this in another section.) Alma taught his son Helaman "that by small and simple things that great things are brought to pass" (Alma 37:6). Make specific, easier, low-level goals your friends.

When you feel like giving up on one of your goals, think about two things. First, **think about your WHY**. If your purpose is well-thought out and meaningful, reminding yourself of your WHY can motivate you to carry on. Second, know that results in the most important things come **after** a lot of time and effort. Too often people give up just before the rewards start coming. It may be hard at first, but believe me, the goals you set and execute will become good habits and good habits are the building blocks of success and character.

Also, don't be afraid to review and change up your goals and plans over time. As a matter of fact, Grandpa highly recommends that you review and revise your goals often. Don't give up on a goal because it's too tough, but as you learn and grow and experience you will see things differently and your needs and strategies will change.

Well-designed plans are multidimensional, with multiple time periods and intensities built in. This means that you may be working on multiple plans at a time and at multiple speeds. Some of them may require an intense, active approach and others may require time and patience. Let me give you some examples. Suppose you find yourself deeply in debt and want to get out. In this case, you need a **short-term** plan that includes changing your lifestyle and **throwing everything you can at the debt until it is gone**. Suppose you want to retire with $2 million dollars in savings. This goal is best achieved by **long-erm, steady and consistent investment over your working career** in a well-planned and balanced set of investments. Can you be working on both of these plans at the same time? Yes! And unless there is some kind of a compelling reason to do otherwise, Grandpa advises it.

I end the discussion on planning, goals and execution, with a caution. Sometimes we can get so focused on financial goals we lose our sense of life balance and this is not good. In one of Grandpa's favorite movies, *Karate Kid*, Mr. Miyagi teaches Daniel San about the importance of balance in karate and in life. This eventually allows Daniel to fix things with his mom and his girlfriend and (more importantly) use the Craine technique to kick Johnny right in the kisser. (You gotta see the movie!)

One time, Grandma Bath took Aunt Celeste and Uncle VJ to her parents' home in Idaho while she recovered from surgery. Grandpa was left alone in our Salt Lake City apartment for about six weeks. During that time, I lived like a miser; turning the thermostat way down, using candles instead of lights, and eating all my meals at my parents' house. I saved a lot of money! It was great! It was only six weeks, but I really believe that if I lived alone, my life would be a lot more like that.

There is **no way** I would try to live like that with Grandma around. She can be tough and resourceful and could make it work, but she would not be happy. Grandpa has learned to temper his enthusiasm and obsessions in many ways because his **most important goal** is to make Grandma happy. Conversely, over the years, Grandma has learned to do a lot of financial things differently because she wants Grandpa to be happy. **Through compromise and balance, we have found a very happy medium!** As you are putting together your financial plan, remember to find balance and you let your financial goals cascade down from your most important life goals.

Chapter 3: Why You Need to Get Money?

Could you live a happy and full life without money? Adam and Eve had everything they needed to live comfortably. They lived in a beautiful, fruitful garden. I don't know if they needed shelter, but they apparently didn't need clothes. They even had a really cool petting zoo. All their needs were filled and they didn't have any money.

What they **did** have was the blessing of work. Work is part of God's plan. Heavenly Father and Jesus set the example of working by planning and planting a beautiful, fruitful garden for Adam and Even. They then placed Adam and Even in the Garden and commanded them to work (see Genesis 1:28 and 2:15). When Adam and Eve were cast out of the garden, they were commanded to work even harder (Genesis 3:17-19).

> **"And the Lord God took the man, and put him into the garden of Eden to dress it and to keep it." (Genesis 2:15)** In this scripture, a better translation of the word "dress" is to "till" (as in plow or weed). Adam and Eve did not just walk around the garden eating fruit and naming animals. They *farmed* the Garden of Eden. They worked!

From that time forth, God has commanded and commended work – it's part of the plan. In 1831, as part of the Law of the Church, the Lord told the Saints, "Thou shalt not be idle; for he that is idle shall not eat the bread nor wear the garments of the laborer" (D&C 42:42). President David O. McKay (1873-1970) said, "Let us realize that the privilege to work is a gift, that the power to work is a blessing, that the love of work is success."

What does this have to do with money? Well, in the beginning hard work brought mankind bounteous crops, an increase in flocks, shelter and warm clothes. This took the labor of the husband and wife and kids because it was wrought directly from the labor of our hands. We farmed the earth, cared for the animals, built the shelter, tanned and sewed the hides. Then we discovered something,

We discovered that some of us were really good at growing crops and some of us were really good at raising sheep and some of us were really good at building shelters and others were really good at weaving cloth and making clothes. And when people spent more time doing things they were good at, they did them even better and faster. Then they could trade the better labor of their hands for the better labor of others hands and everybody lived better. Over time this practice of specialization grew and we started trading for others' labor with the one thing that everybody could trade with everybody – money. So, money, in a way, made life simpler and better.

Grandpa wants you to understand that work is an underlying principle of self-reliance and provident living. You need to work and work hard, and the sooner the better. Once when Aunt Hesper was a little girl she came to Grandpa and asked if she could have an allowance. Playing dumb, I asked her what an allowance was. Her answer was something like, "It's the money you give me so I have money to spend." I looked at her and said, "Nobody pays **me** to live, if you want money go get a job."

Some people would say, she was too young to get a job, but Grandpa disagrees. That's because when Grandpa was that age, I wanted money, so I asked my dad what I could do. He got me some lightbulbs from a distributor and I went around Vernal selling lightbulbs. Over the next few years, I became the town peddler selling light bulbs, event tickets and greeting cards. I never wanted for spending money.

> I didn't just tell Hesper to get a job. I hired her to do chores around the house, for which I "paid" her. I did this with all my children – overworking and underpaying them – but the real payment was that they learned to work. Every one of my children knows how to work.

When I was twelve, my parents wanted to go on vacation to visit Great-Aunt Jacky's family in Louisiana, but weren't sure they could afford it. I found an ad in Boys' Life magazine for pen and pencil sets, sent for and peddled them. I gave the money to my parents and made it possible for us to take that wonderful trip. I got my first "real" job at 15 ½, working as a janitor in a candy factory, but before that, in addition to the peddler job, I mowed lawns, threw newspapers, babysat, worked as an attic money and did odd jobs.

I want you to understand that work is important for you. You need to help around the house starting when you are very young. You need to provide service in the Church and in the community throughout your life. And eventually you need to work to fulfill your own needs and the needs of others.

In our world today, **money** is your reward for working. Money isn't the only compensation you will receive for your work; you will find a powerful correlation between money and your other compensations – including opportunities and respect. It will also affect your self-esteem, your ability to be self-reliant and lift others. Money is evidence that you are willing to work, work hard and do a good job. Money is not everything, but it really is something.

Chapter 4: What Should You Do with Your Money?

Now it's time to talk about the **most important financial question**: What should you do with your money? As I told you in the last chapter, I started making money at a very young age and had a job or ran a business my entire life. I had an innate drive and willingness, but I must give a lot of credit to my parents. They taught me about hard work by both precept and example.

However, beyond teaching me to pay my tithing, my parents did not teach me what to do with the money that I made. That's because they did not know what to do. My parents were teenagers and young adults during the Great Depression, a time in our history when survival was the goal for most people. This made them financially cautious and tentative. My parents worked hard, got by and provided me a good life, but they did not know how to move beyond survival.

I was not satisfied with my parents' attitude about money and felt there was something better. I had dreams of being rich, but didn't have the knowledge or discipline I needed to make that happen. One of the reasons I wanted to be an attorney was that I thought it would make me rich.

And although being rich can be good, I have learned that it is more important to be financially secure. Being financially secure means, you know how to handle and use money. It's **not the way you choose to get money or how much money you make, that makes you financially secure**. It is what you do with your money! Note the irony in the following examples.

- In 2014, a Vermont janitor and gas station attendant, Ronald Read, died leaving almost $8 million to his heirs.
- In 2009, the King of Pop, Michael Jackson died broke and deeply in debt. He owed $500,000 to the IRS alone.

And these are not isolated examples. Almost every day there is a new story of a humble, unassuming person who became rich because they handled their money well, and just as many stories about famous, well-paid people who lost it all. It's all about how you handle your money.

Stanley and Danko spent over twenty years studying how people became wealthy and in 1996 published the book, *The Millionaire Next Door*. It's not about how smart or lucky or driven the thousands of unassuming millionaires that they studied were, or how they made their living. It's about the way those people think about and handle the money they do make.

This is just one of several money books Grandpa has read over my lifetime, and they are only a drop in the bucket compared to the hundreds of books out there that talk about handling money or getting rich. I have read books that contradict each other. I have watched some financial gurus crash and burn, following their own advice. So, who do you listen to?

Remember when we talked about self-reliance and provident living and I quoted from D&C 104 that God wants things done in His "own way"? **This is the key.** The best (meaning safest, most effective and enduring) advice comes from the Lord, his scriptures and words of living prophets. Always square financial advice, even from Grandpa, with His sources.

Let me share an example. When I was a young adult, I read *How to Awaken the Financial Genius Within You* by Mark O. Haroldson. He was a huge proponent of leverage – using other people's money – to invest in real estate. In a nutshell, he advised to borrow big time in order to buy rental properties. Many years later, I read *The Total Money Makeover* by Dave Ramsey. He was a huge proponent of **not** borrowing money **ever** for **anything** – not even your own home if you can help it. Who is right?

Well, it turns out the Lord has given us an answer. This from the Topics and Questions page on the Church's website:

> Since the early days of the Church, the Lord's prophets have repeatedly **warned against the bondage of debt**. One of the great dangers of debt is the interest that accompanies it. When it is **necessary** to incur debt, such as a **reasonable** amount to purchase a **modest** home or to complete one's education, the debt should be **repaid as quickly as possible**. (Emphasis added.)

Remember our discussion on the principle of balance? Here is a perfect example. The Lord's way is to avoid debt in general, but use it **reasonably, modestly** and for as **short a term as possible** – when it is **necessary**. So, whenever anyone (including Grandpa) gives you financial advice, make sure it squares with the scriptures and the words of the living prophets!

Grandpa now intends to give you what he did not have, advice on how to handle the money that you get. These are my opinions, formed from years of study and experience (good and bad), but still my opinions. I will begin, in this chapter, with a short summary of each principle and then elaborate on them in another section.

1. Pay the Lord first

Paying your tithing is the first plank of Grandpa's financial plan. The Law of Tithing is a simple and fair way to show our devotion to God, thank Him for His blessings, and participate in the building of His kingdom. It also comes with great promised blessings.

> Bring ye all the tithes into the storehouse, that there may be meat in mine house, and prove me now herewith, saith the Lord of hosts, if I will not

open you the windows of heaven, and pour you out a blessing, that there shall not be room enough to receive it. (Malachi 3:10 – emphasis added)

I don't know anyone who doesn't want to be that blessed, but I know a lot of otherwise faithful people who don't pay tithing. There are many reasons, but one of the biggest is bad timing. They try to pay the Lord after they've paid their bills and bought necessities, when they don't have enough money left over.

Grandma and Grandpa learned many years ago to pay the Lord just as soon as we get the money. Have we been blessed for this? **Yes!** God has greatly blessed this family and not just financially. I already told you God has bailed me out many times. I never deserved it, but I know God was more willing to extend mercy because I've always paid my tithing.

If you pay your tithing first:

- It will be easier to pay.
- You will be blessed in many ways (including meeting other expenses).
- You will be more disciplined in how you handle your money.
- You will have a better relationship with God.

2. Pay yourself second

Pay your tithing first, but before you buy groceries or gas; make your credit card or car payments; pay the rent or utilities; **pay yourself second.** Many people find this harder than paying their tithing because they want to make sure all their bills are paid on time and because they don't understand the power of saving and investing. They respect God and His laws, and the needs of other people, but they don't respect themselves.

The best way to buy things is to save up for them and the best way to get capital to invest is to save up. The best way to save is to pay yourself second. Be wise! Respect yourself! Build for your future!

Now, Grandpa is going to **shock you a little bit**! I want you to pay yourself **at least** 30% of everything you make.

- At least 10% in short-term savings – things you may want buy or pay for within the coming year.
- At least 10% in long-term savings – things you may want to buy or pay for in the next two years or more.
- At least 10% in investment savings – money you want to put to work for you.

The other 60% is yours to spend as you please and while that may sound like a lot to you, most adults reading this is going to freak a little bit. Let me show you why.

Right now (2024), according to talent.com, the average wage in Salt Lake City is $23.45 an hour and the average full-time paycheck is $3931 a month. The average family size in Utah is right at four people. So, let's see how Grandpa's plan works out for that average Utah family of four living on a **single average** income.

The **chart to the right** shows that after the government takes its cut and the average wage earner pays their tithing; they have $2844 left. That might be enough to cover rent, utilities, food, clothing and transportation – but just barely. And Grandpa says that before they pay for all those things they need to pay themselves 30% of their income. If they do that, they are left with only $1659 to pay the bills. Most adults reading this will say: *You can't possibly save 30% on that level of income.*

Average Monthly Income	$3,941.00
Payroll Taxes (7.65%)	$ (302.00)
Federal Tax Witholding (6.34%)	$ (250.00)
State Tax Witholding (3.8%)	$ (150.00)
Tithing	$ (395.00)
Balance Before Savings	**$2,844.00**
Short-term Savings	$ (395.00)
Long-term Savings	$ (395.00)
Investment	$ (395.00)
Left for Living Expenses	**$1,659.00**

This is an adult problem you do not have to face now, but I want you have a feel for the challenge your parents may have to face. When they nag you to turn off lights you are not using, it might be that they are trying to make a much bigger plan work. Give them some credit for being smart and turn off the darned light when you're not using it.

Let me tell you two reasons I think they're saying that. **First**, they want to be responsible people, good citizens, pay their bills and take care of their family, so they concentrate on paying the bills first. **Second**, saving 30% of their income is not part of their purposeful plan cascading down from their WHY. Remember, I said knowing your WHY would motivate you when things got tough!

Always remember, you are the captain of your own cruise and no one is going to make you pay yourself second. It's only when you want it badly enough that you will find a way to pay yourself second. The good news is I will propose some solutions to this problem in another section of the book.

3. Spend every dollar that you get

Yes, you read that right. You need to spend every dollar that you get.

There are few things more dangerous than a large pile of cash lying around. The old saying goes: "Idle hands are the devil's workshop." That's true, but it's also true that a pile of cash lying around buys the **tools** for that workshop. If you have a wallet, piggy bank, or bank account filled with money it will "burn a hole in your pocket" and you will often spend impulsively on crap. You will be a target for your friends who want you to spend money with them and on them, or they will want to borrow it from you. If you have it in cash, with no way to account for it, it will disappear, get lost, stolen or spent before you can say, "a fool and his money are soon parted." *(Where do you get all these old sayings, Grandpa?)*

I'm NOT saying that you should actually run out and **spend** that money; I AM saying that you should have a **spending plan** for every dollar that comes into your hands. And note what else I did **not** say:

- I **did not** say the word budget. Just like the 80's fitness guru Richard Simmons hated the word "diet" because of its negative connotations, and used instead the phrase "live-it" for his fitness plan, I hate the word "budget." Budgets are forced and limiting, but spending plans are free and fun – we get to spend every dollar we get.

- I **did not** say that knowing where ever dollar is being spent is a spending plan, that's just a really good obsession.
- I **did not** say that spending every dollar means that the money leaves your pocket, piggy bank or bank account or that you lose control. Quite the opposite! A spending plan gives you way more power over your money and makes it more powerful.

The idea behind a spending plan is that every dollar has a place to go and a job to do. It does not leave its post and it does not shirk its duty. It's there when you need it and it has the power to do what you need it to do. And most importantly, it does not try to do another dollar's job.

I am not just obsessed with knowing where my money is and goes; I actually have a spending plan. My spending plan is obsessive but it works well. It has nine income categories and 40 expenditure categories. Sounds like Grandpa is crazy, but every category has an important purpose and there is not a dollar that comes into my hands that does not have

> Grandma Bath teases Grandpa Bath because I insist on balancing my Excel spreadsheet to the penny at least a couple of times a week. She thinks this is funny, but she didn't think it was funny twenty years ago, when I had the same obsession and we were doing it together on a large columnar pad. I would get angry and frustrated when the books didn't balance or when there was a mystery expense or a lost receipt. We discussed each situation loudly and our children actually thought we were fighting – silly kids.

a category and a purpose. My plan was developed over a period of twenty years and fits our family finances very, very well.

Do you really expect your grandchildren to develop spending plans? Absolutely! Without question! Talk about helpful financial ladders, this is one of the **most** important and I will show you how to climb it in another section.

4. Avoid debt like you would a terrible disease

Do you remember what we did to avoid the Covid-19 virus? We stayed home most of the time and when we did go out, we wore masks and stayed at least six feet away from other people. Businesses opened late or closed early so that employees could sanitize everything. And heaven forbid you would have a hay fever attack and start coughing or sneezing in a public place, the glaring looks you got were enough to kill. We feared that disease and acted a little crazy to keep from getting near it.

That is the way Grandpa wants you to act toward debt! Let me tell you why?

- **Debt encourages you to spend more** than you need and more than you can afford. If I go shopping with $50 in my wallet, I know what I have to spend. Handing the $50 bill to the cashier at Target stings just a bit and when she counts back my change, I know part of my money is gone. If I go on that same shopping trip with my credit card in my wallet, it feels like free money, so I am much more likely to buy stuff I wouldn't otherwise. I swipe the card, take the receipt and put in my pocket, but can't tell you how much I've spent. This effect is only amplified with big ticket items. $5000 in cash for a car, becomes $10,000 (spread over 4 years) on credit. $300,000 in cash for a house, become $400,000 (spread over 30 or 40 years) on credit.

- **Debt makes everything cost more**. Not only do merchants pass the cost of credit card and other financing fees on to you in the form of higher prices, credit use also creates money and that money, pumped into the economy, can power inflation.

- **Debt comes with a hidden cost**. That cost is interest and fees. The higher the interest rate and the longer the term, the more you pay. If you pay $5000 cash for a car it costs just that; if you buy it with a 5.5% loan over five years it costs you $5730 (or almost 15% more). If you buy a house for $500,000 with a 30-year mortgage at 7% interest you'll pay $1,197,545 for that house (almost 140% more). Finance companies now offer loans that are interest free for a certain period of time, without any payments. This is still debt and it will come back and take a bite out of your finances eventually.

- **Debt robs your potential**. A debt incurred today, takes money out of your income tomorrow and the next day and the next day, until it is paid off. What could you be doing with that money that has to go to pay debt? Invest? Buy a home? Get an education? Go to Disneyland? These lost opportunities are called opportunity costs and they can be very expensive.

- **Debt enslaves you**. Once you are in its clutches, debt becomes an oppressive task master. It owns you. You cannot move forward in your life because you are chained to it. Not only will debt limit your progress, it will destroy what you already have – peace of mind and confidence.

- **Debt can hurt your credit score.** If you don't plan on using debt, you may not care about your credit score, but your credit score is used for so much more than just borrowing money. Landlords, insurance companies, employers and others often check your credit score to see if you are the kind of person they want to deal with. And you would be amazed how little things, like the overuse of credit for a month or a missed payment or two, can seriously hurt your credit score.

- **Debt can cause** medical and emotional **problems**. Debt can cause you to stress and stress can make you sick. Ulcers, migraines, depression, and even heart attacks have been linked to stress. In addition, stress can cause or deepen emotional problems like depression.

- **Debt can destroy relationships.** Debt will definitely put a strain on a marriage, with money being a factor in up to 40% of divorces, but it can affect other relationships too. Who wants to deal with a friend that is always stressed or grumpy about money or who, heaven forbid, asks to borrow money from you.

- **Debt is seductive.** Listen to these voices. *Enjoy **it** now and pay for it later? The payments are so low and you can have years to pay **it** off. **It** will fit right into your budget.* What is "***it***"? Everything! Entire industries, like advertising and finance, pound us with the suggestion that buying on credit is not only acceptable, but the best way to obtain things. Once we accept that philosophy it overtakes our thinking. When we consider buying something, we no longer think about how much money we have in the bank, we ask, "Can I manage that payment?" And they make it so easy. We don't even have to pull the credit card out of our wallet; it's already on file with all your favorite online retailers. All you have to do is click a button.

I warn you that the world (including friends and family) will not like you bucking the system. Some places will not even do business with you if you don't use a credit card. And people might think you are weird – after all you'll be driving, wearing, eating, buying, using, watching, and enjoying **only** those things you can actually afford, because you know how to use this tool we call money.

You may be asking if there is any such thing as good debt like a home mortgage or student loans or business loans. No debt is good, but sometimes it may be a necessary ladder for you to use. Grandpa will discuss those exceptions in another section.

5. Wake your money up and make it work for you

Saving and investing are two different things. Saving money is good, but investing money is better. Grandpa suggested three savings categories when I talked about paying yourself second. The first two categories help you accumulate money for things you want or need. If you diligently save in these accounts, you will be much more likely to stay out of debt, but the third category is not about buying or spending. **The third saving category is about accumulating capital to invest!**

Capital is **anything** you own that gives you economic value, opportunity or advantage. It is the stuff that you can put to work to create wealth. If you have capital, you can invest in financial instruments and businesses, produce products for sale, provide services for pay, hire people to make money for you, and trade it for other capital.

There are many kinds of capital, but the basic form is money. And although you can borrow, be gifted or inherit money, the surest and safest way to get cash capital is by saving. Once you have saved capital you should put it to work immediately and consistently. It should become **second nature to you**.

Remember when we talked about the slothful steward in the Parable of the Talents. Why was the master angry? **"All I asked was that you do your best. You could at least have put it in a savings account and collected some interest!"** Be a **consistently** good steward of every penny God allows you to get.

Also remember that piles of cash lying around buy the tools for the devil's workshop. Money lying in a checking or savings account can be very tempting, but once it's in a financial instrument like a CD or stock or bond, it is harder to get to and less tempting.

Remember money is a tool to be put to work. At the **very least** your money should be kept in a place that pays you a little, and should be a little hard to get at. But we are not interested in the very least. Your goal should be to accumulate enough capital to put it to work for you BIG TIME. And that happens by doing the small things carefully, consistently and patiently.

There is an old story about a rich rancher and a farrier. The farrier had come to shoe the rich man's horse, for which he usually charged $50. The rich man met the farrier at the stable door and made him a strange offer.

"I am feeling very generous today. I will pay you triple your regular fee **or** I will pay you a penny for the first nail and double that penny with each additional nail. Would you rather have the $150 or get paid a penny doubled all the way through the twenty-fourth nail."

One hundred fifty dollars was a lot of money to the farrier, but he could tell by the look in the rich man's eye that something was up, so he agreed to a penny doubled for each nail. The rich man smiled and said, "Well then my friend, get to work."

The farrier lifted the first hoof, removed the shoe, filed down the hoof, cleaned the frog and then put the first nail in the new shoe. He was already tired when he heard the rich man drop the first penny into a metal bucket and his heart sank, that was a lot of work for just a penny. He had the same sinking feeling when the next four nail payments – two cents, four cents, eight cents, sixteen cents – hit the bottom of the bucket.

As he finished the first hoof, he paused to get a drink and heard the rich man plop thirty-two cents in the bucket for the sixth nail. He did a quick calculation and realized he'd been paid a whopping sixty-three cents for doing a fourth of the job. He wondered if he'd made a big mistake and wondered if the rich man would let him change his mind, but being a man of great character, he decided to stick it out.

He went back to work on the second hoof. As he finished the seventh nail the rich man said, "If you don't mind, I am tired of dropping pennies in this bucket, can I just tell you how much I'm paying for each nail and keep track in this ledger?" The farrier agreed, not wanting to listen to the depressing sixty-four pennies drop, one by one, into the bucket. After the eighth nail the rich man called out "a dollar and twenty-eight cents".

The farrier couldn't take it anymore and put down the partially shod hoof. The rich man was sure the farrier was going to complain, or quit, or ask to renegotiate, but to his surprise the farrier simply said, "Sir, this money thing is a little distracting and I want to do a good job for you. If you don't mind, just keep the record and I will keep my mind on the job."

The rich man agreed and the farrier went back to work, nail by nail; minute by minute; sweat dripping from his brow and rolling down his back. Finally, he was on the last hoof, driving the twenty-fourth nail. He let down the hoof, led the horse around the barn by the halter and presented him to the owner. "Job done," he said.

The rich man simply replied, "$83,886.08."

The farrier looked dumbfounded and sounded even dumber replying, "What?"

The rich man repeated the number and added, "That's one penny doubled twenty-four times. Your total is $83,886.08. Come up to the house and I'll write you a check."

As they walked to the house, the stunned farrier pled with the rich man, "I cannot possibly take that

GRANDPA'S BIG BOOK ON MONEY

much money – all I did was shoe your horse. Please let me take the $150."

The rich man replied, "Oh, my friend, you did much more than shoe a horse today. For you see, I had my young son watching the whole transaction from a perch in the loft. We, today, taught him great lessons that he'll use his whole life."

There are so many lessons that can be extracted from this story, they could fill a book, but for the purposes of this section I want you to take away just two.

One is that your early efforts to save and invest will seem ridiculous. Just like the farrier you will be tempted to second guess yourself, especially when you are only earning a pittance on the small amount you have invested. But as your investment portfolio grows, so will your confidence and security.

> A portfolio is the collection of investments that an investor or fund holds.

Two is that compound interest is one of the most powerful financial forces on earth. Compound interest is when you take the interest you have earned on an investment and reinvest it with the original investment so you are then earning money on **both** the investment and the earned interest. We will talk more about how this works and how you can make it work for you in another section.

6. Buy assets and not liabilities

I am indebted to Richard Kiyosaki, author of *Rich Dad, Poor Dad* for helping me understand assets and liabilities in a unique way. His explanation is very simplistic. As a matter of fact, I'll give you my version of it in one sentence.

Assets put money in your pocket; liabilities take money out!

There is power in that simplicity. And my advice in applying this knowledge in your own financial life is, by extension, very simple.

Buy assets; Don't buy liabilities!

That is about where the simplicity ends and we'll talk about that in another section, but for now I want to make sure you learn and start applying this principle early in your life. **Like right now!**

Here is a bad example from Grandpa's young life. When I turned 16, all I could think about was owning a Ford Mustang. My parents told me it was a bad idea. There were lots of costs involved in owning a car and I could always borrow one of the family cars. But the idea of driving my mom's Rambler Ambassador on a date just did not appeal to me. Great Uncle J.R. was willing to co-sign on a loan so, I went down to Colonial Ford and bought a baby-blue 1965 Mustang for $1000 (that's about $10,000 in 2024 money).

I loved that car and it made me so cool! Even my ex-girlfriend was willing to go out with me again because I owned a Mustang. Few kids in my high school had a cooler car than me. It was great…

…until it wasn't.

You see, four months later I was driving home from work in a freak spring snow storm. I spun out on an icy overpass and smashed the left rear side of the car on a guardrail. No, I had not purchased collision insurance, thanks for asking, so my beautiful car sat in our driveway, undriveable and I still owed $700 on it. There's a lot more to the story, but that's enough to extract a lesson.

There is no question that Grandpa broke the rule and bought a liability. My parents had been right – it was a money pit and on top of that, I bought it on credit and I didn't protect it with insurance.

But Grandpa, wasn't it all worth four months of glory?

Well, that is a very, very good question. Because, you see, the rule isn't, "don't buy liabilities and have a boring life." The rule is "buy assets so that you can get to the point in your finances where your assets provide you a happy, fulfilling life." It's about creating habits and adopting attitudes while you are young enough to make a difference.

> **The funny thing about this story is that my favorite car was not the Mustang. After I sold the Mustang, my dad took pity and spent $150 on a '65 Ford Falcon station wagon for me to drive. My friends and I called it AllShaNoGo (for all show, no go) and had so much fun driving it around. Today, if I could choose between my Mustang and my station wagon, it would be the station wagon.**

7. Protect what you have and love

The saddest part of the Mustang story is that it didn't have to end so tragically. All I needed for a happier ending was collision insurance, but I had not been taught about such things. So, Grandpa wants to teach you about protecting what you have and love, which is great advice for every aspect of your life, but **in this book, we are talking about money** so we'll concentrate on financial risk.

Loss is part of your earthly stewardship and education. Bad things are going to happen to you. But even though you can't eliminate all risk of loss, you can (and should) minimize it. Murphy's Law states: "If something **can** go wrong, it will!" This may sound pessimistic, but when it comes to minimizing risk, a little pessimism is a good thing. Immature people don't think about risk and it often comes back to bite them. If you don't believe me, watch a few Fail Army videos. Mature people don't **obsess** about risk, but they do what they can to assess risk, prevent risk and put plans into place to recover from loss. Grandpa will say much more about this subject in another section of this book.

8. Be generous with your riches

It is important that you make a habit of sharing your wealth, including your money. You may be tempted to believe that being generous will make financial independence more difficult, but the opposite is actually true. Studies have shown that people who are generous with their time, money and effort are healthier, happier and do better financially. Being generous also serves as a magnet for good people to come into your life. And people who make an effort to be regularly and consistently generous develop habits and attitudes of success. These facts are not surprising considering 3000 years ago the Lord inspired King Solomon to counsel:

> A generous person will prosper; whoever refreshes others will be
> refreshed. (Proverbs 11:25, NIV)

While all these benefits of generosity are wonderful, the best reasons for giving should be love for your fellow man and gratitude to God. Remember that nothing you have really belongs to you – it's all God's. You are just His steward. And when the opportunity comes to help any of His children, you should take it. Grandpa leaves you with this promise. Helping others with your time, money and effort will bring you more joy and blessings than just about anything else you can do. We will talk about how in another section.

Tots to Teens: Milestones in Financial Independence

Age 0–4

Welcome to the world! Grandpa doesn't expect much from you at this time in your life. About all I would expect is that you learn to control bodily functions, walk, talk and count to 10. Oh, and have fun!

Age 5

Okay, you are a big kid now. It's time to start learning about making choices and how to delay gratification. Have your parents give you the opportunity to choose between choices that are acceptable to them rather than tell you what to do. For the rest of your youth, as you get better at making good choices, your parents will give you more choices. Have your parents teach you about delayed gratification (the opposite of instant gratification) and give you the opportunity to practice it. Have them challenge you to give up some things now for bigger or better somethings later or save up for something you want. Have them break tasks down in to kid-size steps and use visuals like timers and calendars to make waiting more tangible. Have them start with simple challenges and work up to bigger ones and ask them to be patient with you as you learn.

Age 6

It's time to start earning and learning about money. Have your parents teach you what the different coins and paper money bills are worth and how they are related. The best way to do learn about money is to have some to save and spend. Earn money by doing **regular** chores around the house or for neighbors. Pay your tithing first, and then pay yourself second, by creating three savings buckets (labeled canning jars work great). Put 30% of your earnings and windfalls into these buckets. It won't look like much is going into your jars at first, but the important thing is to develop the habit. At this age, don't put more than 10% in each bucket because it all about balance – have some fun with your 60%.

Age 7-8

You're old enough to start understanding the WHYs of money, Grandpa's Big Book of Money (GBBM) will help with that. Have your parents help you read and understand chapters 1-4. Have them share it with you in kid-size chunks and be creative as they teach it. Make sure you understand that money is just a tool and how it is used. Learn the difference between wants and needs and how so much of **their** money goes toward needs. They may want to let you have some input into how some of your family's household money is spent – like putting you in charge of bringing down a utility cost or letting you make choices about buying your school clothes. By now, you should be an "old hand" at earning money by doing chores regularly and your jars will have accumulated savings and investment money. This would be a good time to open a custodial savings account at a bank or credit union and start putting your savings and investment money in interest-earning accounts.

Age 9-10

You have come a long way! You understand the basics of money. You've been earning, saving and spending your own money. Don't obsess, but be sure to regularly check on how your money is doing in the bank. It's now time to start thinking things through and make some plans. Although you will not finish this project for many years, you're old enough to **start** planning out your life. Learn goals in **Chapter 5: Subsection One** of GBBM and practice making and executing some simple life goals and plans (buying Christmas presents, getting straight A for a semester, learning to play the banjo, etc.) Over the next couple of years, you'll start working on more serious goals and plans like starting a business or side hustle, getting an education and investing. Another thing you should start doing at this age is keeping records. Start a journal and write about your life, record your goals, plans and progress and keep track of your money. Consistent and diligent journaling may be difficult at first, but keep working at it. Keeping good records is one of the most important skills you can master.

Age 11-12

Now that you have had some experience earning and handling money and designing and executing plans, it's time to put those skills to work. Using a plan, you develop and with your parent's (or older siblings) help, start your own business or side hustle. I am talking about more than just a one-and-done lemonade stand here. Make it something you can be proud of and pursue for least a couple of years. This will be more about gaining experience than making a lot of money and your parents should make sure you have the complete experience (see the four steps outlined in GBBM **Chapter 5: Subsection Two**). Record keeping becomes even more important when you are running a business. Set a goal to have at least $100 in each of your "buckets" by the time you turn 12.

Age 13-14

Read GBBM **Chapter 6:** *Subsection Five* and put together your first investment plan and investment team (you and your parents). Set up your first custodial brokerage account. Between your chore money, windfalls and money from your business or side hustle, you could have a substantial amount to invest (especially for a 13-year-old), so put it to work. Practice ignoring your investments and letting them grow, but keep an eye on them and keep good records. From this point direct your pay-yourself-second investment money into your investments as soon as possible.

Age 15

You've got a lot on your plate with a side hustle and investments and this is the age when you should get serious about school – academics and extra-curricular activities. Concentrate on getting good grades, and learning to take the ACT and SAT, because these things can have serious economic advantages for you. Also, be involved and have fun. Starting at age 16, life gets much more serious. Don't give up on the things you've been doing, but let's not add anything to your plate this year except a re-read of the whole GBBM book.

Age 16

Hope you enjoyed your year "off", because things are about to ramp up. Adulthood is right around the corner. Keep up with school, but now you need to find (or create) a job. At the very least you need a summer job, but I recommend you fit in a part-time job (or your ramped up side hustle) during the school year that accommodates your schedule. If you get a driver's license, you'll have a lot more freedom and opportunity, but remember (as my Uncle Ben once told me) with great power comes great responsibility. Remember to pay the Lord first and yourself second. More of your money should be going to long-term savings for college, mission and don't forget to put at least 10% into investment. Oh, and your parents will need help paying for gas and additional insurance costs when you start to drive.

Age 17-18

Remember when you were 6 and Grandpa told you to enjoy the 60% leftover after paying the Lord and yourself? Well now at age 17, I take it back. With your parents paying for almost everything in your life, the next two years are your opportunity to sock some good money away before launching. So, get (or create) a good job, work hard and think more like a F.I.R.E. follower than a 6-year-old. As an almost adult you have to keep up with everything Grandpa has put on your list and get serious about your life and financial plans you started way back at age 10. Also, this is the time to finish up strong with school, extra-curricular activities, community service and college and scholarship applications. If it's too much, prioritize and drop off the things that are least important (even if that is making money).

Young Adulthood

If you have followed Grandpa's advice to this point, you will have a really, really solid financial foundation to build upon. Now that you are an adult and charting your own course, you'll have some opportunities to learn and serve that will not easily come your way again. This is the time for missions, military and community service, and post-secondary education. If you have done your planning, saving and investing you'll easily be able to afford these. Take the time to serve and learn, however the Spirit directs you, even if that means putting financial concerns to the side for a couple of years. Even if it means dipping into your savings (I **did not** say investment funds). College or trade school are important, but don't have to be expensive. And for heaven sakes don't go to college just for the experience – what a waste of time and money.

For at least part of this time, you may be living away from home. This will be your first real taste of adult financial responsibility and the principles in this book will become very real for you. Follow them from the start. Some of you will be invited to live with your parents during part of young adulthood and if you accept that invitation, I want you to do three things:

1) Be grateful, cooperative and obedient. Yes, you are an adult now, but it is their home and they have the right to expect certain things of the people who live there.

2) Pay them rent. Your parents will most likely charge you significantly less than you'd have to pay a money-grubbing landlord and they are not likely to evict you if you miss paying for a month. They may give you the opportunity to "work off" your rent by taking on extra chores and duties around the house and that's fine, but if they offer you free room and board, decline. Under no circumstances are you to mooch off your parents. Work out some way to pay them.

3) Take this opportunity to sock money away in savings and investments. You'll hear this spiel from A LOT from me in GBBM so I won't elaborate. You know the drill.

Chapter 5: How Should You Do with Your Money?

The title of this chapter is a little weird, but it is very accurate. This is the first *"another section"* I alluded to all the way through the previous chapters. In previous chapters I covered the WHYS of personal finance. The rest of the book covers the HOWS. There will be a lot of detail and some technical jargon.

Unless you've really bought into and given some serious thought to the WHYS, this section may not click with you or it may seem a little boring. You may be excited about all of this and ready to really dive in, **or** you not be ready at all and that's okay, because everyone is different. My purpose for writing this chapter is to give you the benefit of my learning and experience **when you are ready**. It's seriously okay to take a break.

If you are at (or ever get to) the point in life where you want to know HOW, the rest of this book will give you some seriously powerful suggestions. That may be now, or when you have made a few mistakes and need to reset. Also, you can read and study it all the way through or use it as a reference book, it's up to you. To facilitate using this part of the book as a reference, I have divided this and the next chapter it into sub-sections.

- Chapter 5 is divided into:
    - Subsection One: How do I create a financial plan?
    - Subsection Two: How do I get money?
    - Subsection Three: How do I handle money?
- Chapter 6 is divided into:
    - Subsection Four: How do I avoid debt like the plague?
    - Subsection Five: How do I put my money to work?
    - Subsection Six: How do I buy assets instead of liabilities?

Lastly, this book is written to prepare teenagers and young adults to be financially successful. An eleven-year-old could take this information and run with it, but so could a sixty-year-old. The principles are universal and timeless. The earlier you learn and apply this stuff, the better you will be able to take care of yourself and your family, help others and be a powerful influence for good in the world. Money is not everything, but it really is something.

Before we launch into the HOWS, **let's review what we've learned.**

- This book is based on these undergirding principles.
    - Money is just a tool.
    - Everything belongs to God and we are His stewards.
    - You are your own cruise director.
    - There is a correct way to climb a ladder.
    - There is power in self-reliance and provident living.
- Wise personal finance requires good planning and good execution.
- Work is an important part of God's plan and money is the reward the world gives you for work.
- It's not how much money you make, it's what you do with it.
    - Pay the Lord first.
    - Pay yourself second.
    - Spend every dollar that you get, through a spending plan.
    - Avoid debt like the plague.
    - Make your money work for you. Be consistent, patient and compound the returns.
    - Buy assets; not liabilities.
    - Protect what you have and love.
    - Always be generous with your riches.

Subsection One: How do I create a financial plan?

Earlier we talked about having a navigational tool for your financial journey called a financial plan, and that a good plan is made up of a set of well-thought-out SMART goals that cascade down from and support your purpose. Let's talk about how you do that.

First, you need to know what a goal is. Here's a great definition from *Preach My Gospel: A Guide to Missionary Service*, under the heading "How Do I Use Time Wisely."

> Goals reflect the desires of our hearts and our vision of what we can accomplish. Through goals and plans, our hopes are transformed into action. Goal setting and planning are acts of faith.

A goal is a declaration of faith that something you hope for can really happen. You are not just wanting it; you are taking the first step to making it happen. For example, if your eleven-year-old self wants to buy your mom a nice Christmas gift (purpose), you tell yourself that you will save half of your chore money every week until you have saved $10 (goal).

Second, you need to understand how goals cascade down from your purpose and how goals are related to and support each other. The goal to save half your chore money until you have saved $10 is a very simple goal – just perfect for the simple purpose of an eleven-year-old. But adult-level goals are rarely that simple. Most of the adult purposes are supported by different levels of goals that are interrelated and support each other.

Here's an example. Let's suppose you love the idea of **being a high school history teacher**, and want to find a way to support your **additional desires of having a big family and providing a fulfilling and quality life** for them. Financially, this will be tough to do on a high school teacher's salary, but you feel it's your calling in life. You now have a purpose. Let's design a plan to make this happen.

To begin with we should do some research; talk to educators to see how they do it; consult trusted advisors (like your parents or school guidance counselors); think deeply and pray. For right now, just take a few minutes to think about how you could make this dream happen.

I'll wait!

While I was waiting, I brainstormed and came up with my own ideas:

- **Get a masters and doctorate to maximize you position on the teacher salary schedule.**
- Learn to coach a sport or extra-curricular activity to supplement your income.
- Gain a marketable skill that will allow you to make a good supplemental income.
- **Learn skills that will allow you to provide products and services for yourself** (auto mechanics, plumbing, electrical, carpentry, **woodworking**, cooking, gardening, husbandry, seamstress, canning).
- Teach in a state/school district that pays well.
- Teach and live in a rural area where the cost of living is lower and there is less socio-economic pressure to keep up with the Jones.
- **Have a business or source of residual income that supplements your income.**

These may not be the best ideas, because I didn't do any research or spend much time at it. You could do better if you really worked at it. but for the purposes of seeing how adult-level goals build on each other, we will go with **the three strategies** that I've boldel on the list.

From our three chosen strategies we can extrapolate examples of top-level, mid-level and lower-level goals and show how they work together. We will use the graphic on the next page.

[I want to give credit for the idea for the graphic to the authors of the BYU-Pathway Connect Life Skills course – which, by the way, I totally recommend to all of you.]

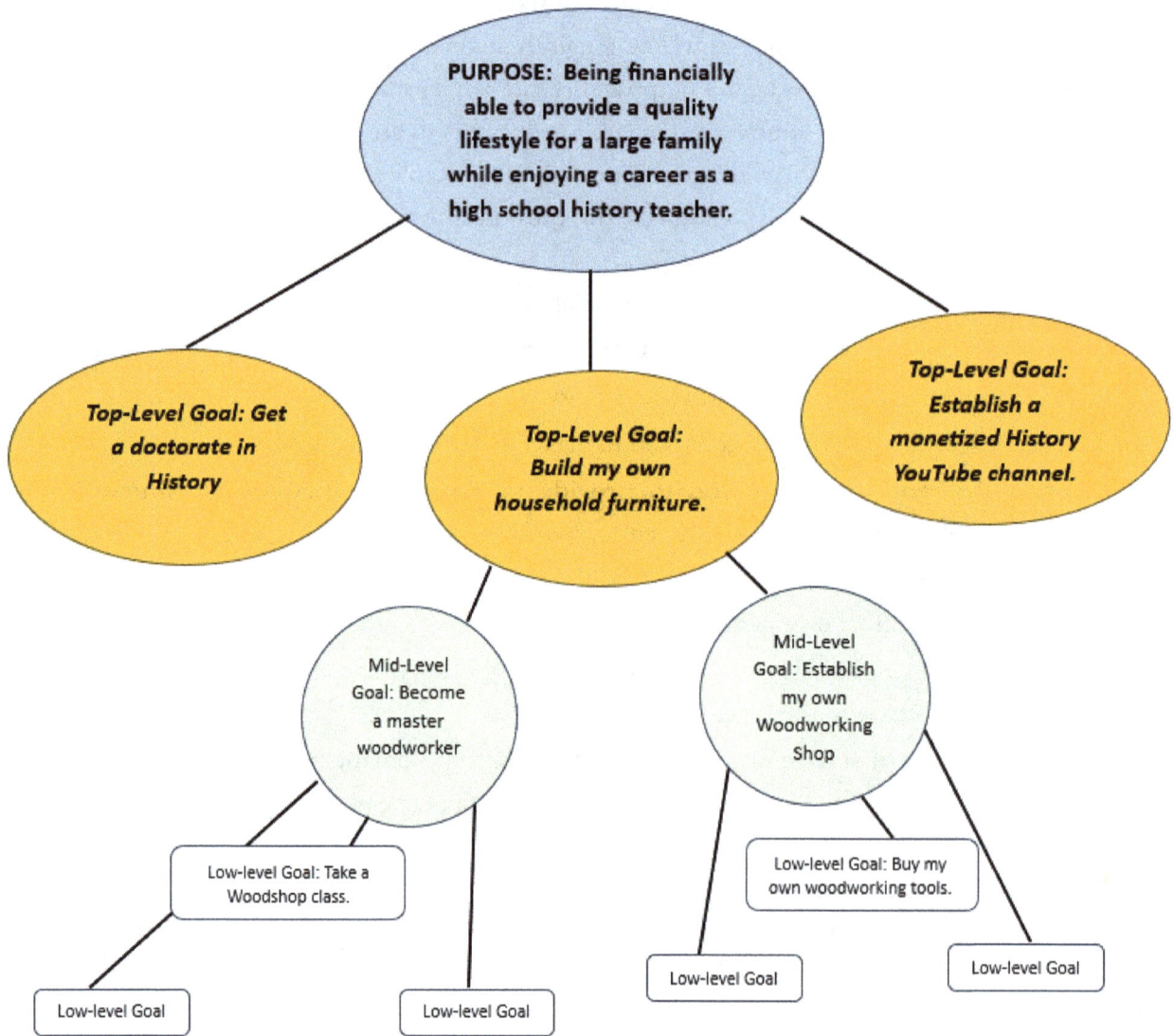

PURPOSE: Being financially able to provide a quality lifestyle for a large family while enjoying a career as a high school history teacher.

Top-Level Goal: Get a doctorate in History

Top-Level Goal: Build my own household furniture.

Top-Level Goal: Establish a monetized History YouTube channel.

Mid-Level Goal: Become a master woodworker

Mid-Level Goal: Establish my own Woodworking Shop

Low-level Goal: Take a Woodshop class.

Low-level Goal: Buy my own woodworking tools.

Low-level Goal

Low-level Goal

Low-level Goal

Low-level Goal

Any of the goals found in the orange ovals could stand alone as a purpose, but in this case, they are **top-level goals** because they cascade down from and support our purpose in the blue oval. **Mid-level goals** (green circles) are more specific than top-level goals, breaking them down into more manageable steps. Then our **lower-level goals** (white rectangles) break our mid-level goals down into even more manageable steps.

Third, we need to get smart with our plan. What we have done so far gives us the skeleton of our plan, but now we have to put flesh on it – refining our goals into powerful tools called SMART goals. SMART is an acronym for the five elements a powerful and effective goal should have.

- S is for specific. Your intended results and steps to get there should be specific.

- M is for measurable. Your goals should be objectively measurable.

- A is for actionable. Can you really achieve this goal? Is it within your ability? Do you know anyone who has accomplished a similar goal?

- R is for relevant. Does this goal support your purpose and help you to achieve higher goals? Does is serve a purpose in your life?

- T is for Time Bound. When are you going to achieve this goal and what are your intervals for measuring your progress.

Now we will take our low-level goal from the graphic above "Take a Woodshop class" and turn it into a SMART goal. It will read: "I will take Mr. Johnson's Woodworking class as an elective Junior year and complete at least two major projects."

- Specific: Tells **when** (junior year), **from whom** (Mr. Johnson, because he's an excellent teacher); **how many** (two major projects).

- Measurable: Contains two measurable elements – **number of projects** (two) and **scope of projects** (major).

- Actionable: If you've never done woodworking before, two major projects might require extra time and effort, but it can be done.

- Relevant: This goal cascades down from your purpose and your top-level goal of learning to build household furniture and is one of the steps in support of your mid-level goal of becoming a master woodworker.

- Time Bound: It is going to be done during your junior year. The class is free in high school and you have time, senior year, to learn more woodworking before you get busy with college.

Now, this goal is more powerful and will help propel you where you want to go! Now let's apply what we've learned and set a *__financial__* goal as part of a plan.

Let's suppose your 16-year-old self thinks it would be cool to be an engineer. At the outset, this is just a wish, but as you think about your WHYS it becomes more. You talk with your parents, teachers and guidance counselor and they strongly agree that you'd make a good engineer. You learn that engineers are well compensated for their work and have more opportunities. You feel that, as an engineer, you'd not only enjoy your work, but be able to support your family well, inspire your children and help your fellow man. You're really good at designing and building things and learn that those skills are important in engineering. After some thought and prayer, you feel inspired to be an engineer.

Your wish has become a purpose.

You put forth more effort to learn what it takes to become an engineer and learn:

- Engineers need a strong foundation in math, physics, chemistry and computers.

- Engineering degrees from an accredited university cost, on average, $50,000.
- Engineers often work in teams and need to have problem solving skills.

You take what you learned and develop some top-level goals, one of which is financial. **I will prepare to finance a $50,000 college education.**

Wait! Did I just read that right? Did you really say that a 16-year-old was setting a goal to finance a $50,000 college education?

Yes, yes, yes! I'm sure a lot of you just fell off your chairs, but this is a **very** plausible goal for a 16-year-old. *How is she going to pull that off?* The same way she would eat an elephant – one bite (mid and lower-level goal) at a time. Let the following illustration illustrate.

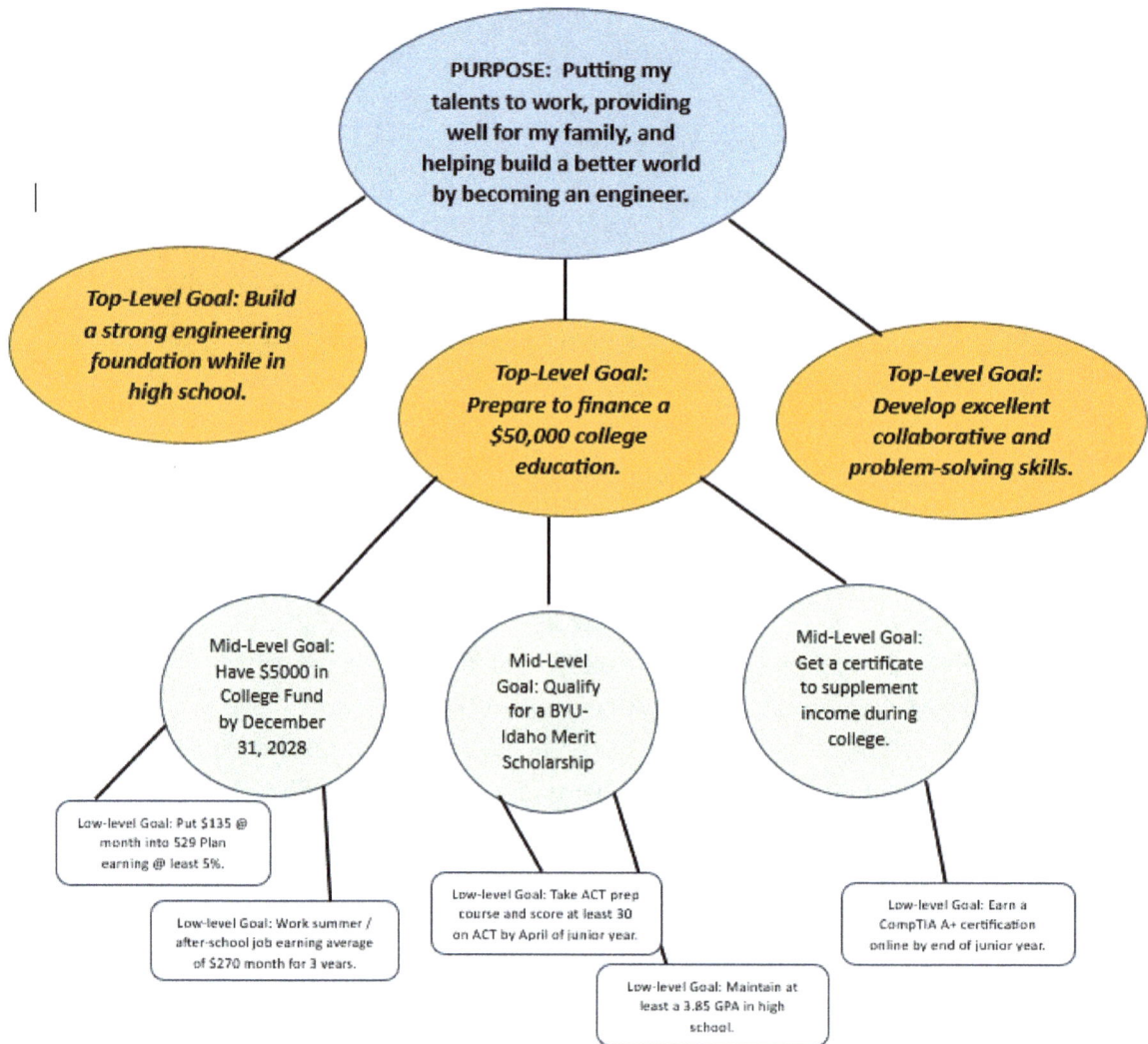

Do you see it? The top-level goal of "preparing to finance a $50,000" college education cascades down from and supports the purpose. It is more specific than the purpose, but not yet a SMART goal.

The mid-level goal "qualify for a BYU-Idaho Merit Scholarship" cascades down from and supports the top-level goal. It is even more specific that the top-level goal, but still not SMART. The low-level goal of "take ACT prep course and score at least a 30 on the ACT by April of junior year" cascades down and supports the mid-level goal, but it is SMART?

- Specific: Tells **what** (ACT score), **how** (prep course), **when** (April, junior year), **how much** (at least 30).
- Measurable: **Minimum score** of 30.
- Actionable: A 30 on the ACT is ambitious, but you can take it early and often and a prep course will really help. (Besides, you are my grandchild!)
- Relevant: This goal cascades down from the purpose of "becoming an engineer" and your top-level goal of "preparing to finance a $50,000 college degree" and is one of the steps to supporting the mid-level goal of "qualifying for a BYU-Idaho Merit Scholarship."
- Time-bound: It's due spring / junior year. This is plenty early to go on your college and scholarship application and is early enough in case you need to take the ACT again.

So, let's answer some of your questions about what we just did.

Q: Could these low-level goals be broken down even further?

A: Without question and it could be helpful. The smaller the bites the better.

Q: Could I be working on more than one goal at a time?

A: Without question and unless there is a compelling reason not to, you should be.

Q: Won't following this plan put a kink in some of my other plans and activities?

A: Without question, so you need to be careful, seek counsel and strive for balance.

Okay, those were easy questions. Do you have any tougher ones?

Q: This ACT low-level goal didn't say anything about money; how does it qualify as a financial goal?

A: The goal does not mention money, but remember what I said about work. It takes work to get a 30 on the ACT. And, if you have at least a 30 on the ACT and a GPA of 3.85 or better, BYU-Idaho will award you a full-tuition scholarship and that my grandchild is money in the bank.

Q: What if I do to all this work and then decide not to go to BYU-Idaho or change my mind about becoming an engineer.

A1: An ACT of 30 and a GPA of at least 3.85 will qualify you for a scholarship at many colleges and universities. It may not be full-tuition, but it will still be money in the bank.

A2: The very act of achieving such a lofty goal is a reward in itself.

Q: What if I fail?

A: This question sounds like it came from the slothful steward in the Parable of the Talents. Yes, you could put a lot of effort into this goal and only partially achieve it or even fail miserably. But at least you will have tried and by trying you will gain wisdom and confidence. You would be a better person just for trying and that my grandchild is a real education.

Q: Isn't all of this thinking, research, planning and goal setting a lot of work?

A1: Yes!

A2: The key to financial success is work. You either work harder or smarter. Smarter will bring you more success and will, in the long run, be easier and more fun. All of this thinking, researching, planning and goal setting is working smarter.

A3: It looks like a lot of work to someone who has not done it before. The more you do this kind of smarter work, the better you will become at it and you may even find it easy and fun. Start now and learn to do this. Start with easier goals and work your way up.

> Don't know what you want to do when you grow up? This is okay, lots of people change their minds in college and later in life. But don't waste time and money figuring that out. My advice: Choose something and go for it, work hard and do your best at it. If you find out you hate it or like something better, you can switch to the new discipline. The knowledge, expertise and experience you gained along the way can, more often than not, transfer to your new discipline.

You now know how to design financial plans and goals, but remember that a **plan is only as good as it's execution**. Here are some keys to actually working your plan.

- The better the design, the easier the execution. Most important elements in design: strong purpose, cascading and supporting goals, lots of small bites.

- Believe in and remember your purpose. Your WHY will keep you going.

- Track your progress. Tracking your progress will keep you accountable and visualizing your progress will motivate you.

- Show some grit. No secret sauce here, just dig down deep when the going gets tough and find that inner strength. (Fasting and prayer, priesthood blessings, counseling with parents, Church leaders and good friends – all these things help a lot.)

- Adjust your goals. It is not okay to give up, but it is okay to adjust your goals on account of changing circumstances or miscalculation.

- Take help and support. Hopefully ask for it, humbly take it, be grateful and pass it on.
- Celebrate your progress. Set milestones and throw parties when you reach them.

Subsection Two: How do I get money?

It is really difficult to become financially successful if you don't make money. At least I've never met anyone who has done it. Even people who inherit fortunes or win the Lotto, can go broke pretty fast if they don't figure out a way to make that money work for them. So, let's talk about making money.

1. When should I start making money

You should start making money as soon as possible. Besides having money to spend, it teaches you so many life lessons. People will give you excuses for not being able to make money throughout you life–being too young is only one of many, but ways do exist and at a very young age. You know my story about being the town peddler and, yes, that was a different time and place (today, people wouldn't let their eight-year-old son run around town unsupervised like that), but in my opinion, there are MORE opportunities for very young people to be making money today than ever before – especially with help from parents or older siblings.

Let me give you just one example. In our city, the Boy Scouts used to do the flag fundraiser. They would contract with people in their neighborhood to post an American flag in their yards on patriotic holidays and they made a killing. When the LDS Church left Scouting in 2019, thousands of troops in this city ceased to exist – leaving that service market totally ripe for the picking. It wouldn't take much to fill that need and make some serious money working maybe 10 days a year. Just sayin'!

Teenagers should have no problem making money and should do it. If you need some brainstorming help, check out *Appendix A: 101 Gigs, Side-hustles and Businesses for Youth* in the back of this book. You need to balance your money-making efforts with school, church, activities, family and friends, but making your own money as a teenager is a sign of maturity and it looks great on college and scholarship applications.

2. Who should I work for

Having established that you should be making your own money as early in your life as possible, we need to talk about who you should work for. I never said you need to get a job; I said you need to make your own money. To do that you can either 1) work for someone else, (2) work for yourself or, best of all, (3) make money work for you.

I once heard a presenter say that if you work for someone else, you're stupid. He was biased, trying to sell his listeners a self-employment opportunity, but what he said stuck with me and I have thought a lot about it over the years. I've come to the conclusion that working for someone else can be a very wise thing to do. The **good news** is that when you work for someone else, they assume the liability and costs involved in the endeavor. All you need to worry about is getting to work on time, working your shift and doing a good job. The **bad news** when you work for someone else is that, because they want to make a profit after all their expenses, they will only pay you what they

FLIPPING BURGERS Let's suppose you get a job at a fast-food place. The owners provide the building, the utilities, the grill, shake machine and other means of production. They pay for all the supplies you need to make and serve the food. They get the business license, insurance and buy advertising. They buy software and computers and/or hire professionals to take care of the money, payroll and taxes. They deal with vendors, repairmen and inspectors. And when it comes to hiring you specifically, they pay for your training and uniform, buy workman's compensation insurance in case you get hurt on the job and pay half of your payroll taxes.

think they can afford. Your liability and costs are limited, but so is your earning potential.

There is also good news and bad news involved in working for yourself. The **bad news** is that being successfully self-employed takes a lot of initiative, hard work and some of the best results come only after a lot of time and effort. You can't give up. The **good news** is that self-employed people have the potential to make a lot of money after the dust settles. **More good news** is that starting your own little side hustle does not require a lot of capital or legalities and you don't have to pay taxes until you've made $400 or more in yearly profits.

Having your money work for you is wonderful. The **good news** is you can put it to work and walk away and let it generate income. You don't have to deal with the hassles of the workplace or of owning or running anything; you just go about your life. Of course, I am talking about investing your money. This sounds rosy, but there is some **bad news**. There can be some risk involved. You can lose some or all of your money if an investment goes bad. Second of all, you have to have money to invest and since most young people are just starting to make money, we'll put a pin in this for now. But don't forget it; it should be your ultimate financial goal. We will talk about the HOW of investing in a later subsection.

So, is it better to work for yourself or for someone else? The answer is: **Yes!** It depends on your particular circumstances and what you want. The important thing is that you do something – even if it's wrong.

3. Why did Grandpa just say that

The hardest part of anything is getting started. **Once you start you will find it much easier** to take the next step and then the next step and then… For two and a half years before I got my first "real" job, I delivered newspapers. I got out of bed at 5 AM and threw about 75 to 100 newspapers **every** morning – rain or shine. But before I could deliver the papers, I had to go to the drop-off point, read the manifest to see if I had any starts or stops, fold the papers and bag them if it looked like rain. I also had to collect from the customers every month, because the money that was left over after I paid for my papers, bags and rubber bands was my pay. (Think *Newsies!*)

When I first started throwing papers, Great-grandma Bath got me up and drove me around *every* morning. She came up with the idea of putting a stamped, self-addressed envelope in the fold of each paper toward the end of the month so most of my customers mailed me their payment. She drove me around and waited in the car (kind of my enforcer) while I collected from the delinquent customers. I could never have done that job without my mom's help and she never even asked me to pay for gas.

> Twenty years after I had that paper route, I became bishop of a ward that was part of my route. One of my ward members, Sister Service, never once referred to me as her bishop. She always introduced me as the best paper boy she ever had.

As time went on, I became more independent. When weather permitted, I delivered the papers from two huge bags hung on the handlebars of my Schwinn. I confidently approached the deadbeat customers. And the last summer I threw papers, I not only took care of my route, but also my brother Larry's afternoon paper route while he was back in Arizona.

> To be totally honest, when you are making money as a youth, you are (in one way or another) getting a lot of help from your parents. They will be willing to help and you should take that help and be very grateful. They recognize their efforts in your money-making endeavor as an investment in your growth and future. To quote my friend the Mandalorian, "It is the way!"

My point? Even though my paper route was hard, with my mother's help I grew into it and became very, very good at it. So, whatever you decide to do while you are young get your parents help and support and you can grow into the job.

One of the lessons gleaned from Richard Kiyosaki's book, *Rich Dad, Poor Dad* is the idea that **you should work to learn, not to earn**. There are many aspects to this philosophy and you should really read the book to get them all, but for today take this away. Youth is a wonderful time to work to learn and it doesn't really matter if you work for someone else or for yourself. Since you don't have to worry about providing the necessities of life, you can concentrate on learning from your job or your business ventures. (And I strongly suggest you try both.) Pay attention. Ask questions. Take notes. Use your work experience to gain skills, develop your talents, and learn what you're good at.

If you face struggles, learn from them too. Is your boss a jerk? Fantastic! Learn what not to do as a boss. Did you get fired? Yea! Figure out what you did wrong and don't do that again. Was your business venture a colossal failure? Do it differently next time.

4. How do I get a job

There are two steps to getting a job. One is to find a job opening and the other is to get hired. It's not as easy as it sounds, but if you follow my advice is will be easier.

In the last century people used to look for jobs in the **Help Wanted** section of the newspaper, but very few employers use newspapers anymore. Now they post to online recruiting platforms, jobs boards, trade or professional journals, social media platforms or classified sites. These postings are a vast improvement over old help wanted ads for several reasons.

They are timely. Because employers can post, edit or remove their posting in a few moments, there are almost no significant delays. You can be relatively certain that a posted job is a real need that is still open.

They are detailed. An online job posting can tell you so much about the requirements, skills and duties of a job. This helps you to know if it's the kind of job you want, if you are a good fit for the job and how you can promote yourself for the job.

They are convenient. You can learn about the job and apply for it in minutes, from the comfort of your home, while lounging around in your pajamas. Applications completed electronically so you can copy and paste your responses, add photos, edit and include your resume from your computer and you don't have to worry about your penmanship.

The Internet is not the only place to find job openings. You can check out the job board or talk to a career counselor at you school, go to an employment agency, or attend job fairs. But by far, the **most effective way to find a job opening is to use your network**. In 2023, the U.S. Bureau of Labor reported that 70% of all jobs are found through networking. In other words, asking people you know for a job or job referral.

In the broadest sense, your network is everybody you have made a connection with – relatives, friends, teachers, Church leaders, neighbors and the friends and acquaintances of all of the above. How about the guy standing behind you in the checkout line at the convenience store? Well, how badly do you want a job? While I wouldn't rule out asking everybody you know and come into contact with for a job recommendation, realize that not all networks or job asks are equal. The better the network and the better the ask, the better the result.

The best networks are people you have developed a rapport with. Who will be more likely to recommend a job to you (or recommended you for a job), the advisor to your school club who you've helped with several projects or the teacher whose class you ditched several times to take extra-long lunches? Wise people work hard at developing positive relationships with a broad range of people, treating everyone they know with respect and doing it long before they need their help. Strong positive relationships are the basis of a strong network.

> **In case you didn't know, employers and college admissions committees often check out prospective applicants' social media posts to see what kind of a person they are. Just sayin'!**

This is a great time to talk about social media. Sometimes social media takes a bad rap because if it is misused it can cause problems or be dangerous, but just like money, if it is used wisely, it can be a great tool. And that includes being a great tool for networking. If you connect with a broad range of good people, treat everyone with respect and keep your posts positive and uplifting, you will have created a helpful network when you need help.

In addition, you need to know the best way to ask for a job referral. This is where your **elevator pitch** comes into play.

[Grandpa is now going to steal some excellent instruction from the BYU PathwayConnect 102 curriculum on *Networking and Interviewing* and the *Find a Better Job* course offered from the Church's Self-Reliance Services.]

A "Me in 30 Seconds" statement is exactly what it sounds like – a brief, prepared and polished summary of who you are and what you need, delivered in about thirty seconds. It is sometimes called an **elevator pitch** because you can deliver it in the time it takes you to ride with someone up an elevator. It can be used to ask for a job referral, in job interviews, or on your résumé.

Here are the key elements in an effective Me in 30 Seconds statement:

- Name
- What Job You're Looking For
- Why You're Good at It
    a. Qualifications
    b. Example

- Asking for Specific Help (see examples below)
    a. Who would you recommend I talk with?
    b. What opportunities do you know of for someone like me?
    c. What businesses are in the area that are looking for _____ (job type or position)?
    d. Who do you know who does what I want to do?

One of the reasons that this formula works is that it clearly connects what you're looking for with what you are good at so that when you ask for help, people can quickly figure out how to help you.

The best job Grandpa had while in high school was selling shoes at Gallenkamp in the mall. I worked there for almost three years before my mission and another couple after I came home. I got the job because a girlfriend's father, who sold shoes at another store, liked me and thought I'd do a good job. He actually talked to a shoe-store manager friend of his about me before I even applied. With his recommendation, I was a shoe-in (pun intended) for the job.

My girlfriend's father was in my network and I didn't even have to ask for his help, but if I had, my elevator speech might have read something like this:

> "Mr. Lee, Patty tells me you sell shoes for J.C. Penney. I'm interested in sales as a possible career path. I'm a fast learner and very good with people. You can often see me starting conversations with people I've never met at the gas pump or checkout lines. Do you know any retail businesses that are looking for an ambitious salesman?"

Grandpa has watched a lot of little Cub Scouts make similar pitches selling Scout popcorn. It worked because few people could resist the little Cub Scout in his uniform and squeaky voice – I called it the **cuteness factor**. An elevator pitch is the adult version of the cuteness factor – but it's more like the **sharpness factor.** People can't resist a sharp person, appropriately dressed and groomed, delivering an elevator pitch. They will **want** to help you.

Once you've found a job opening, you only have one more thing to do – get hired. The best way to get hired is to figure out what your prospective employer needs and convince him you are the fulfillment of that need.

If you are referred by someone in your network, you already have a "foot in the door" but don't take the job for granted. Learn everything you can about the employer and what they need from your friend, from the employer's website and job postings. The more you can find out beforehand, the better you'll do in the interview and as you start the job.

Most often, a job posting is your best source for knowing what an employer needs. Remember that I said modern job postings are detailed? A good posting will list the requirements, skills and duties of a job. These (ta-da!) are the employer's needs.

Let's suppose you are looking for a part-time job. You play soccer on your high school soccer team and really love the sport, so when you see a job posted for a part-time soccer coach in your area, you get excited. I pulled an actual job posting off the Internet and put it on the next page. Take a look at it and see if you can figure out what the employer needs.

I'll wait!

Youth Soccer Coach for After School Elementary Classes

ARE YOU PASSIONATE ABOUT WORKING WITH KIDS AND LOOKING FOR A FUN PART TIME ROLE?

Super Soccer Stars has been in the youth soccer business for over 22 years and have been recognized as the largest operating program in the U.S. We are looking to hire an ==energetic and fun-loving== Soccer Coach who will lead our children in fun and educational activities while ensuring ==safety== for all. Our ideal candidate ==has prior experience working with children== (as a sports coach, teacher, camper or leader). This position is excellent for someone who has an interest in pursuing early childhood education, or child development. New Coaches can work 5-10 classes a week and can earn from $18 to $25 per hour.

- Our Coaches use ==individual attention to== ensure ==every child== has success
- Our Coaches use a ==non-competitive approach== to ensure classes are fun with a stress-free environment
- Our Coaches use ==positive reinforcement== to encourage children to do better and celebrate success
- And finally, our coaches have a blast. They are ==open-minded==, and know that coaching is a continuous journey. All Coaches are ==open to feedback and strive to be better== by attending ==regular trainings== and following the Super Soccer Stars Coaching Manual

Responsibilities

- Teach and coach children age 2-10 in a fun, educational, and non-competitive environment
- Provide positive reinforcement and feedback to children during class
- Monitor and maintain a safe environment for children
- Communicate effectively with parents and other staff members
- Attend and actively participate in training sessions and meetings
- Set up and take down equipment before and after classes

Requirements

- Must have ==excellent verbal communication skills==
- Must be able to work in a fast-paced environment with children
- Must be available to ==work flexible hours, including weekday afternoons, evenings, and weekends==
- Must pass a background check
- Must ==have current CPR and first aid certifications or be willing to get certified==.

Benefits

- Flexible schedule based on your availability
- Coach referral program for every coach you recommend
- Work with a top-notch national coaching organization that provides all the tools and training needed to be successful.

Okay, I cheated! While you were reading through the job posting I highlighted items I think are the employer's needs. They need an employee that…

- … is energetic and fun loving.
- … is safety conscious.
- … has prior experience working with children ages 2 to 10.
- … able to give individual attention to every child.
- … can use a non-competitive approach and positive reinforcement.
- … is open-minded, open to feedback and willing to improve.
- … is willing to attend training.
- … has excellent verbal communication skills.
- … is willing to work flexible hours, weekday afternoons, evenings and weekends.
- … is CPR and first aid certified or willing to become such.

After seeing all these expectations, you might not be comfortable applying for this job. It sounds like they want a superhero for $18 an hour! Novice job seekers may look at this list and be discouraged, thinking they couldn't possibly qualify. You probably don't meet all of these qualifications, but this employer would probably be shocked to find someone who did.

The **good news** is you probably meet some of the requirements, and more than you think. You love and know soccer and have experienced playing and being coached. You can think of examples from your life where you have tended or supervised young children; been a positive person and built other people up; learned to take constructive criticism and apply it? Have you taken speech or debate in school? Do you love to learn and are you excited about learning to coach and do CPR? See, all of a sudden you are preparing to flesh out your resume and kill an interview.

And that is **better news**. Knowing what the employer wants, allows you to tweak your résumé and practice for a job interview. This is not cheating. This is not bragging. This is emphasizing your best self and making killer impressions.

For example, let's say you are in an interview for this job:

Interviewer: Tell me about one of your weaknesses.

~~Somebody Else's Grandchild: Well, I really have never coached a soccer team before. I guess that could be a weakness as far as this job is concerned.~~

My Grandchild: Although I have never actually coached soccer, I've played on recreational and school teams and had lots of coaches. I've loved the enthusiastic, fun coaches that were positive and built me up. I loved those that gave me individual attention and helped me build skills. I look forward to being trained in your system and becoming that kind of coach from the start.

Wow! You just blew that interviewer out of the water. You knew what the employer wanted and told him, in essence, you were clay in his hands to be molded into the best soccer coach ever – this is the **sharpness factor at work**. And you didn't have to come up with that answer off the top of your head, you wrote and practiced that response before you ever came to the interview and it is a stock answer you could have used to answer a number of standard interview questions.

Now, there is a lot more to writing a résumé and preparing for a job interview. Grandpa will not give you detailed

> Find out more about the Church's self-reliance courses at **ChurchofJesusChrist.org/self-reliance**

instructions here because he is tired and it is his nap time. Okay, the real reason is that there are a lot of excellent sources for learning how to write a great résumé and preparing to kill a job interview that do a much better job than Grandpa can do. Too often we don't take advantage of these resources until we are struggling. I highly recommend that you search out these helps and make them part of your youth and young-adult education. I especially endorse the self-reliance courses and materials developed by the Church – they are magnificent.

But in wrapping up *How do I get a job* let me emphasize a few things I've learned from experience, both as an employee and employer.

Writing a résumé:

- Find and use a résumé template that both looks sharp and is easy to edit. Practice with it so you can edit it quickly and easily.

- Write a boilerplate résumé that includes a lot of detail and covers all your experience, education and training. You will **not submit this**, but you will cut and paste it to create a new résumé for each job posting designed to emphasize how you can meet the employer's needs.

- You have just ten seconds to catch an employer's attention, so your résumé should be easy to read, eye catching and a maximum of one page long.

- Learn to use power statements and emphasize your skills and experience. (They will teach you how to do this in the resources I mentioned above.)

Interviewing for a job:

- Prepare a list of questions you think the interviewer may ask and write out an answer to each question. Those answers should emphasize your skills, abilities and willingness, and how they fill the employer's needs.

- Practice your answers over and over again in front of a mirror.

- Prepare a few questions of your own to ask during the interview that show you are curious and hopeful about the job.

- Dress one step up from what you think will be required of the job and make sure your clothing is clean and pressed.

- Be well groomed – clean and smelling good.

- Be right on time – not too early and definitely not late.

- Make eye contact throughout the interview. If the interview is over Zoom, making eye contact means looking directly into your camera.

- Speak clearly and loudly. Offer a brief, firm handshake if prompted.

- The correct answer is "yes" or "no," not "yeah," "yep," "naw," "nope," or any other type of slang or grunt.

- Display a positive and enthusiastic attitude about yourself, the job and your interviewer.

- Always speak positively about former employers, jobs and co-workers. This includes explaining why you no longer work there. This should be a prepared and practiced answer.

- When the interview is over, thank the interviewer for their time and ask what the next step will be. Respect the interviewer's time and leave promptly.

- Ask about pay, benefits and other logistics **after** you are offered the job, but before you accept.

5. How do I start a business or side hustle

Why would you want to start a business or side hustle? The obvious answer is to make money, but you can make money working for someone else, often for less effort and hassle. So, there has to be some other compelling reasons. Let me share some of Grandpa's favorite WHYS for starting a business.

- **Running a business or side hustle gives you freedom and control**. If you can't find a job or don't like any being offered, make your own. If you have something you love to do, profit from doing it. If you want to work when you want, be your own boss.

- **This is a great opportunity to meet people** – both customers and other business owners. Getting to know and learning to deal with others are great skills. You will see the good, the bad and the ugly, but in my opinion, small business owners are some of the best people you will ever meet. They have a great work ethic, understand what it takes to make a profit and are often very generous with their time, money and advice.

- **One of the best ways to learn and gain expertise** in almost any field is to run a small business in that field. You either learn and grow quickly or your business dies. Even a business failure is a great lesson.

- **There is a great sense of accomplishment and fulfillment** that comes with making your ideas come to life. It can do wonders for your self-esteem, even if you fail.

- **Owning a business can widen your circle of influence.** Business owners often have a wide circle of friends and acquaintances. They are also highly respected in the community.

- **You not only can make money in business; you can make a lot of money**. Your upward potential is not limited by what your boss is willing to pay, but by how hard and smart you are willing to work.

- **Owning you own business give you control over the here and now and the opportunity to carve out a better future** for you, your family and your community. And that "tomorrow" comes much more quickly that you can imagine.

- Channeling your energies into your own enterprise **can be a fun and creative outlet** for your passions. It can **also offer relief** from frustration and emotional pain.

- **Being self-employed has some great tax advantages.** Often you can reduce your tax burden by deducting business purchases that otherwise would just be expenses. You will benefit from this advice much more when you are older, for now, just learn how it works and develop the right habits.

- **A business or side hustle can be a hedge against instability.** Even if you have a good job, in a good economy and a bright future, things can change and having an operating advocation can be a great help.

Even if you have a job, I recommend that each of my grandchildren establish at least one small business or side hustle of some kind, even if it's only for the educational benefit. And if jobs are scarce or child labor laws prevent you

> Don't forget to check out *Appendix A: 101 Gigs, Side-hustles and Businesses for Youth*

from entering the work force yet, I highly recommend it. So, the next question is how does a teenager or young adult start a business or side hustle. Here are the steps I recommend.

Step One: Decide what you want to do or sell. This sounds simple, but it is really a very important, if not the most important, step in creating a successful business. It's not enough to say, I like doing or making **something.** You have to ask yourself if people want your **something** and how your **something** will be different so people will want it. Sometimes the best **something** may be **something** people can't (or don't want to) do or make for themselves.

The other day as I was working on this book, three boys came down the street with a pooper scooper and a large shopping bag. They were offering to pick up the dog poop in people's yards for $5. Unfortunately, we had just picked up the dog poop in our own yard or we would have hired them, because we **hate** picking up Charlie's droppings. I would gladly have paid them to do it and, as a matter of fact, I would pay them $5 every week to come do it. We told them we would hire them next time and I really hope they come back. This is exactly what I am talking about. If they got a good steady clientele and spent 15 minutes per yard, they could really clean up (pun intended), making $20 an hour.

I don't know where they got this idea, but even great flashes of inspiration **need to be researched**. How do you do that? Well, there are two types of market research, primary and secondary. Primary research is original research you do yourself. Secondary research is research others have already done. This may sound boring and difficult, but it doesn't have to be.

Let's use our young pooper-scooper entrepreneurs as an example. Their primary research could have been a survey created on Google Docs and emailed to friends, neighbors and family. Or they could take a walk around the neighborhood and look for houses that have dogs in the yard, knock on those doors and ask if the owners were interested in the service. They were actually doing this the day I met them.

For secondary research they could google "who will pick up my dog poop?" I did this just now and found at least seven different companies that clean dog poop in my area. I also found that they charge at least $12 for weekly service for one dog and the price goes up from there.

Wow! Market research for their business was not boring or hard. And let's suppose they found quite a few people wanting this service and that people are paying $12 a week to have it done regularly. Would you think they would be onto a good business idea? I do!

That takes care of step one.

Step Two: Create a business plan. This means you think carefully about how you are going to make your business work and write it down. This is one of the times your parents and other mentors can be a great help. Questions you will want to answer with your business plan include:

- Who will my customers be and where will I find them and serve them?
- Where and when will I run my business?
- What skills and knowledge will I need to successfully run my business and where can I learn them?
- What supplies and equipment will I need to run my business?
- Which of these supplies and equipment do I (or my parents) have and which do I need to procure? What will it cost me to procure them?
- How much are my startup costs (enough money to get started and operate until I make money from my business)?
- How much will it cost to make and deliver my products or provide my service?
- How much will I charge for my products or services (enough to cover costs and make a profit, but not so much that it discourages people from doing business with me.)
- How much do I expect to make, especially compared to the amount of money, time and effort I put into the business? (This is called return on investment or R.O.I.)
- How will I promote my business and find customers?
- What will I call my business?
- What are the goals for my business? (This would be a good time to review what I 've taught you about making plans and setting goals.)

Once you have your plan down on paper, run it by your parents and mentors and get their feedback. If you're a minor, get your parents approval and secure their help. When your plan is ready, you are ready to move on to step three.

Step Three: Figure out how to fund your business. The startup costs for the scooper business are virtually nothing. To get started you would need a scooping device and some shopping bags and your parents probably have that stuff lying around the house anyway. It might be a good idea to have some flyers made up to advertise and remind customers "who they're going to call – poop scoopers!" You can probably make those on your home computer for the cost of paper and ink. Other than that, your costs are going to be your time and effort.

Lots of businesses (especially service businesses) get started this way. Are your parents willing to let you use their lawn mower and grass trimmer; you're in the lawn care business. Is there a power washer in your garage; you're in the power washing business. A dog walking business? Your customers will already have the leash. If you can drive the family pickup truck, haul junk to the landfill for your neighbors or start recycling metal.

If your business is successful (you're making money and gaining customers) you may need to maintain, repair or replace your equipment and replenish supplies. You may choose to upgrade or expand your equipment or hire some help. These decisions all need to be made carefully and with the help of parents and mentors.

Some businesses require some funding to get started. We call this capital. And where do you get this capital? There are basically three ways – 1) borrow, 2) partner with an investor, or 3) invest your own money. If you borrow, you are indebted and have to pay the money back with interest – whether your business makes money or not. If you get someone to invest in your business they are assuming part of the risk of loss, but they are entitled to part of your business and/or profits. If you use your own money, all the business, risk and profit belong to you.

Some considerations:

- Remember R.O.I. If you are going to put a boatload of money into a business, you'd better be sure it will make two boatloads of money back. It's better to start conservatively and grow.

- Also, it's easier to borrow money or find investors if your business is already operating and making money.

- Most youth and young adult businesses will not require loans. If yours is an exception, whomever lends you the money will want to see two things.
    o They will want to see that your business is likely to make money so that they can get paid back with interest. This makes your business plan much more important.
    o More importantly, they will want to see (via your credit score, income and assets) that you can pay the loan back with interest. They may even ask you to put up collateral.

> Collateral is something you own that lenders can take and sell in case you default on the loan.

- Your parents are more likely to be able to get the loan or may choose to cosign for you. Cosigning means they become joint borrowers with you and will have to pay back the loan if you don't.

- Investors will be most concerned with R.O.I. **and** will want to know that you will follow through on you plans and make things work. Also, they will want to know how much of the business they will own and how much of the profit they get to keep. They will also want to know how they can get out of the deal and what they can do if the business fails.

- All the details of loans or taking on investors should be worked out and put in writing before any money changes hands. If your investors are anybody other than your parents, you probably need to consult an attorney.

At this point it may seem like Grandpa is purposely piling on difficulty to discourage you from borrowing money or looking for investors. That would be a good strategy, but Grandpa doesn't need to do that. There **is** a lot to consider. As a matter of fact, Grandpa has only scratched the surface of all there is to consider and take care of if you go either of those routes. Grandpa's preferred advice for funding your business would be to save and invest your own money. This keeps things simple. You are a sole proprietor, assuming all the risk and owning all the profits. You will also, most likely, have to start small and grow, which is a great way to go.

> **STARTING SMALL AND GROWING?**
> - **Patrick McDonald started a humble food stand in Monrovia, CA in 1937. His sons later moved the building to San Bernardino and that became the first McDonald's.**
> - **At 17, Fred De Luca started a sandwich shop with $1000 borrowed from a family friend. That grew into Subway.**
> - **In 1939, Bill and Dave started building audio oscillators in their garage. Their company is called Hewlett-Packard (HP) today.**
> - **Phil Knight started Blue Ribbon Sports with a $50 deposit on Japanese-running-shoe samples. He showed and took orders for them from the trunk of his car. Blue Ribbon became Nike.**

This is even more true (and possible) today than it has ever been. That is due mostly to an amazing invention called the Internet. Here are some of the ways the Internet makes starting and running a business so very easy for young people.

- **You can start a business at almost any age.** At age 4, Mikaila Ulmer started selling Honey-bee lemonade. At age 7, Aline Morse started selling sugar-free Zolli Teeth Cleaning Candy. And at 11, Maddie Rae developed and started selling Slime Glue. These are all real big-time, revenue-producing businesses with customers around the world, thanks to the reach of the Internet. Google them.

- **Your client base is almost unlimited** – we are talking billions of potential customers. Somewhere, out there on the Internet are people who want your product or service. Your only limitations are your ability to produce and deliver.

- **If you own a computer and have Internet access, it costs very little to start or promote your business on the Internet.** Your major costs will be for supplies, equipment, travel and delivery. And like I said, start small and grow.

- **Social media provides you an amazing marketing tool** and, again, it is basically free to use.
- **You can conduct business from anywhere** you have Internet access.
- **You can find supplies and equipment at great prices** on the Internet and they will be delivered right to your door.

Grandpa is not writing a book about starting a business on the Internet, but you don't need one. The **College of Google** and **University of YouTube** will **teach you how do almost anything** related to your business – for free.

> That wise man was Chinese philosopher Lao Tzu who actually said: "A journey of a thousand li [a Chinese mile] starts beneath one's feet"

Step Four: Get started. Like the wise man once said, "The journey of a thousand miles begins with a single step." Grandpa has given you a lot to do to prepare to launch a business, but getting started made be the hardest task for some of you. To help, I offer these inspired instructions. 1) Take a step. 2) Repeat as often as needed. Okay, here's my real advice.

- Ask your parents, family and mentors for help.
- Manage your time wisely so that you have time to conduct business and so that the business does not take over your life.
- Review your goals often and make adjustments as needed.
- Celebrate the milestones in your business and reward yourself for doing well.
- Market yourself. This is where social media can really be a great tool.
- When you make mistakes fix them and learn from them.
- Keep careful records of income and expenses and detailed notes on how you operated. Your parents and mentors can help you with this.

This is all I'm going to say about starting and operating a business. I do hope you will give it a shot and, succeed or fail, let me know how it goes.

6. What if I am not a teenager anymore

You may be reading this after you've become an adult and, feeling adult pressures, wonder if any of this will be helpful to you. Yes, I've geared this book to the child and teenage you, trying to get you a head start. **I hope you took it**. But what if you didn't. Is it too late?

Let me guarantee you that everything I am teaching in this book is universal and timeless. It is never too late to start practicing the principles of provident living and self-reliance. As a matter of fact, the older you are and the more responsibilities you have, the more important they are. So, continue to read and, as you do, make the adjustments that will make this work for you.

The one thing I would add if you are learning and starting to apply this in adulthood is that you need to move past jobs, side hustles and gigs and either start a real business or get a career. Grandpa really doesn't care what you decide to do to get money, as long as it is legal and moral and it provides for your needs. The specifics of career and business development are really beyond the scope of this book, but I do have some suggestions for you.

- Be serious about your search, decision and preparation.
- Use the many resources out there including the Church's Pathway Connect and Self-reliance courses, college, university and apprenticeships programs.
- Talk and listen to your parents – they have a wealth of experience and are experts on you.
- Instead of focusing your career on your passion, focus on what you are good at and work to fill a need that you may uniquely fill.
- Find a mentor, someone who excels at what you choose to do, and let them guide you.
- Be flexible and willing to follow both the promptings of the Holy Ghost and opportunities as they present themselves.
- As with everything in life, money is something to consider, but it's not the only thing or the most important thing.

It is Grandpa's belief that his careers have been guided and shaped by Heavenly Father. I know he has guided me and he will do the same for you if are prayerful and humble.

Subsection Three: How do I handle money?

As soon as you start getting money, begin handling it properly, keep handling it properly and always handle it properly. The wisdom of following the principles outlined in this subsection is the same whether you make $10 a year or $10 million a year. **Do not let rationalization or procrastination rob you!** Thinking that you don't make enough money to worry about these principles will keep you poor. Waiting to apply any of these principles until you get yourself established will prevent you from getting established. Believing that you make so much money you can afford to ignore these principles will waste potential.

1. How do I pay the Lord first

As outlined in a previous chapter there are many good reasons to pay your tithing and pay it first. I don't feel the need to re-teach the WHY of this principle, except to say, "What kind of a fool would NOT want God on his side?"

What I do feel the need to teach is the HOW of tithing.

To begin with, you need to gain a personal testimony of the principle of tithing. You may have been paying tithing all your life, but take some time to study this law and pray to know it is a true principle. Then commit yourself to paying a full and honest tithe.

You should pay your tithing as soon as you can, immediately if possible. Setting the money aside – either physically, electronically or on a spreadsheet – is not paying your tithing. Get it out of your hands and into the hands of the Lord's servants as soon as possible to avoid loss, error or temptation.

Organize your life so you can pay you tithing ASAP. For example, if you pay your tithing in

Church on Sunday, keep a stack of envelopes and tithing slips at home to make up your donations. Also, ask a member of your family to remind you to give your tithing to the bishopric so you don't forget and take it home with you. If you use electronic banking, establish a donation account on the Church website so you can pay electronically from your bank account.

Make tithing a part of your financial planning and thinking. For example, when you are buying a home, your maximum home mortgage payment should be 33% of your gross income. However, wise tithe payers take into account the fact that they pay the Lord first and deduct 10% from their gross income before calculating their maximum mortgage payment. The maximum mortgage payment **before tithing** on a $7500 monthly income would be $2475 a month, but the maximum mortgage payment **after tithing** would be only $2228 a month – about a $250 difference.

Exercise faith and gratefully receive the blessings of tithing. Just paying tithing does not entitle you to temporal blessings, but they will come as you exercise faith. And paying a full and honest tithe will increase your faith. It will be easier for you to approach God and His servants for help. Then, when you are blessed, be grateful and work to help others.

When I was serving as bishop, a couple asked me if they should pay tithing on their **gross income or net** income. I told them, "Yes!" That is because I consider tithing a personal commandment. Your promise to pay a full and honest tithing is between you and the Lord.

> Gross income is the total amount you get paid before deductions. Net income is how much you get after deductions (taxes, benefits, etc.) are taken out.

When conducting a worthiness interview, your bishop will simply ask if you are a full tithe payer and you will answer "yes" or "no." If you prayerfully approach the Lord, he will inspire you. Follow that prompting.

If I could only give you one piece of advice on how to handle your money, it would be "Pay a full, honest and timely tithing!" I testify that my efforts to pay a full and honest tithe have been rewarded both temporarily and spiritually. I also testify that over the years my willingness and ability to pay have increased.

2. How do I pay myself second

In a previous section, I recommended that you pay yourself **at least** 30% of your income – 10% each to short-term savings, long-term savings and investment. If you are reading this as a teenager or a young adult still living in your parents' home, this will be very easy for you. Just do it and perhaps save even more. Get in the habit and make it part of your financial DNA so that it carries over into adulthood when living this principle becomes more challenging.

If you are young, the suggestions I am about to give to help you pay yourself second may make little sense or be way over your head. I may use terms you don't understand. You may not even be able to relate to what I am saying. **But I don't apologize at all!** You need to hear this as early as possible and as often as possible in your life. Why?

It is because of all the pieces of advice I will give you in this book, paying yourself second these may be the **most difficult** principle for you to grasp and follow. However, I believe that this principle is the **missing link** that most people lack to be financially successful. Master this and you'll have a **significantly** greater chance of being financially independent, self-reliant and secure. Here is HOW to pay yourself second.

The first step is to have respect for yourself. This is often hard for us. We see the value of God and everyone else around us, but we often place ourselves a distant third. This is a mistake! You deserve to get paid second. You need to pay yourself for taking care of the thousands of things that make up the business of life. If someone does these things for you, **they** expect to get paid. You work hard for yourself and deserve to get paid for it. You have great potential to make the world a better place. Paying yourself second helps you become more independent, self-reliant, secure and realize your potential.

The second step is to overcome the thinking errors that prevent you from paying yourself. We **think** that to be honest and trustworthy we must pay our bills first so we don't run out of money. Change that thinking. Yes, it is important to fulfill your obligations, but if you have a hard time paying your bills after paying yourself second, you either have too many bills or aren't working hard enough. We **think** that there is something wrong if we (or our dependents) have to go without. Change that thinking. Sacrifice and delayed gratification are great character builders and I say that with the straightest of faces. We should take action if we are going without **necessities** after paying ourselves second, but luxuries are a different matter, usually a matter of pride. And you would be surprised to learn what Grandpa considers a luxury. We **think** that paying ourselves second is nice. Change that thinking. Paying ourselves second is a vital imperative. It will make or break you.

The third step is to solemnly promise to pay yourself second and then do whatever it takes to keep that promise. All of the suggestions I make hereafter are offered for the purpose of helping you keep this promise to yourself.

Once you start having respect for yourself, correcting your thinking and really committing to paying yourself second, the pieces start falling into place. The following suggestions will be helpful to prime your intellectual and emotional pump, but the best ideas will come from your mind, your heart and from your relationship with God.

Here are Grandpa's suggestions:

- **Get your pay out of your hands and into savings and investments ASAP.** Most payroll services, banks and credit unions have auto-deduction and deposit services, so contributions to saving and investment accounts can be paid directly from your check, before you even see it. If you do not get a regular paycheck or are self-employed you will just need to practice self-control and be systematic about it. And remember it needs to go into accounts that are **at least** a little hard to access so you won't be tempted.

- **Reduce your tax withholding**. The government requires your employer to take some of your pay and send it to them to cover your income taxes at the end of the year. (If you're self-

employed you have to do this by making quarterly deposits to the IRS.) This is called withholding. The **bad news** is that most people get too much money taken out and have to ask for the money back. **More bad news** is that the government doesn't pay you any interest on your money they are holding. And **even more bad news** is that most people see the tax refund as some kind of a windfall from a benevolent Uncle Sam, so they run out and spend it. The **good news** is that you have some control over this. Using one of dozens of reliable online worksheets, you can pretty closely estimate what your taxes will be and instruct your employer (with a new W-4) to just send the government that amount. Pay yourself with the rest.
Some cautions:

1) Put this money into an interest-bearing account or instrument until you file your tax return for the year. That way, it will be there if you've underestimated your tax liability.

2) If you do underestimate and have to send in a **big** amount, you may have to pay a small penalty.

3) If you are an independent contractor or self-employed you'll manage your own quarterly withholding payments.

- **Reduce or defer your actual tax** bill. There are **many** ways to reduce or defer your actual taxes. This requires study, planning, record keeping and careful choices on your part and, sometimes, the help of a tax professional.

  o You can defer or reduce taxes by **investing in government approved plans** designed to invest for your future. **Imagine that!** They include:
    - Qualified Retirement Plans (401Ks, IRA's or Annuities)
    - 529 Education Plans
    - Health Savings Plans (if offered by employers)

  o **Schedule A deductions** like medical expenses, charitable contributions and mortgage interest can reduce your tax bill if they are more than your standard deduction. When you're young, you'll most likely always take the standard deduction, but you should learn to keep careful records of your expenses so you'll be in the habit when you may qualify to take the greater itemized deduction.

> Tax deductions are amounts that you spend, save or invest that the government allows you to deduct from your income before you calculate your taxes. You can either take a **standard deduction** (set amount) or **itemize your deductions** (add up all of your deductible expenses) – whichever is greater.

  o **Expenses incurred in starting or running a business** (or side hustle) can be deducted from your taxable income. Learn to keep careful records.

  o **Certain investments allow you to make money and not have to pay taxes on that money.** These include earnings on municipal bonds; EFTs and mutual funds made up of municipal bonds; Roth savings accounts; and certain life insurance products.

- **Reduce your expenses**. It's simple: spend less and pay yourself more. Expenses fall into two categories – necessities and luxuries. Necessities are things like food, shelter, clothing, utilities, transportation and healthcare. Luxuries are everything else. **Necessary expenses** can be reduced in so many ways I cannot even begin to list them all. But to get your intellectual pumps working I suggest an activity. Take the following necessities and think how your household could possibly reduce their cost.
  - ○ Food
  - ○ Shelter and Utilities
  - ○ Clothing
  - ○ Transportation
  - ○ Healthcare.

  Luxury expenses are even easier to reduce because they are not necessary to keep you alive or out of jail and that is pretty much Grandpa's definition of a luxury. You will be surprised what you can live without.

- **Increase your income**. One of the advantages of paying yourself second is that it motivates you to find ways to get the bills paid. This is where second incomes, part-time jobs and side hustles come in. The **good news** is that they can be powerful tools for achieving your goals and grow into something more than just a temporary fix. The **bad news** is they come at a cost (time, sleep, health, family relationships) and you need to make sure the money is used according to your plan and the principles laid out in the beginning of this book.

- **Play games with your money**. Learning to pay yourself can actually be fun. One way to make it fun is by playing games with your money. If you go to Las Vegas and… No! Not those types of games. I am talking about little ways you can tweak your finances. Let me share some we play.
  - ○ **Skim money off every electronic transaction**. Every time I spend money; I round up the purchase to the nearest dollar (in my books) and pay myself. Every time I make a deposit or get a refund; I round down (in my books) and pay myself. Each transaction is less than a dollar, but they add up. Playing this game, I added over $300 to my Christmas fund in 2024.
  - ○ **Pay with cash**. Grandpa seldom uses cash, but Grandma loves it. She can hold it, count it and spend it. One of the advantages she reports of paying with cash is that it is a touchable and tangible reminder that she is spending money. Feeling that money leave her hand makes her less likely to spend or overpay when she spends.
  - ○ **Toss spare change into a jar.** When Grandma cleans out her purse, she throws the change into a jar on her dresser and forgets about it. This is a cash version of skimming electronic transactions. By the way, Grandma's last trip to the bank

(after about a year of filling the jar), netted her over $60 to hold, count and spend.

- o **Smashing aluminum cans in the garage.** Another fun thing about Grandma is her substance abuse problem. She is addicted to caffeine and feeds her habit with caffeinated drinks that come in aluminum cans – sometimes 3 to 4 a day. Grandpa makes a game of this and collects them (everyone else's soda cans, beer cans I find in parking lots, etc.) in a designated bucket. About once a week I take them to the garage, smash and collect them in a big garbage can. I don't make much money when I take them to the recycler (a little over $25 a year) but it's better than throwing away money. (By the way, each aluminum can is worth about a penny and a half).

- o **Sharing a meal.** When Grandma and I eat out, we make a game out of how we can share a meal. We do this because restaurants portions are often so large, one person cannot eat it all. That food usually goes home in a "doggie bag" but seldom gets eaten and this is waste (which Grandpa hates). The money side of this game is that we can often dine out very cheaply.

Those are just of few of the ways we play money games. None of them, by themselves, will make us rich, or even make a huge dent in our finances, but we play them because collectively they do make a difference; they keep us thinking frugality; and they make managing money fun.

- • **Ask for help**. Everyone needs help at one time or another. When you need it, ask for it, take it and be grateful. Help can come in many forms, but the best help is temporary, designed to help you maintain your dignity and help you become self-reliant. Go to your family first, then to the Church and, when appropriate, go to charities or the government. Don't misunderstand me. I am not suggesting that you go "on the dole", but don't be too proud to ask for and take help when needed.

I would like to end this discussion on How to pay yourself second with some important thoughts. First of all, remember that it is your mind, heart and inspiration that will come up with the ideas you need to pay yourself second; these suggestions are only primers. Second of all, your plan to pay yourself second needs to be manageable and sustainable. It should hurt, but not cause undue or irreputable harm. **Balance** is the key. When you marry, being equally yoked on these principles with your spouse will get you further and faster than you can imagine.

3. How do I spend every dollar I get

My parents rented a home in South Salt Lake for almost nine years. Every month like clockwork, they wrote out a check for the rent and mailed it to their landlord. One day they got a call from a lawyer who represented their landlord's widow. The landlord had died two years earlier and the lawyer was helping his widow straighten out his estate. The landlord's widow was a Korean war bride who spoke little English and did not really understand how finances worked. Her husband had taken care of all that.

The lawyer explained that the widow had taken my parents' rent checks for that last two years and instead of depositing them in the bank, she saved them in a cigar box. Now, a check is a promise to pay that a bank only has to honor for six months after it is written. So, technically this widow had a cigar box full of worthless checks.

How in the heck did my parents not know their monthly rent checks were not being cashed for two years? They worked hard, saved money and paid their bills on time, but they obviously did not have a handle on their money. If they weren't even reconciling their bank statement with their checkbook, they obviously didn't have a spending plan.

What is a spending plan? I am glad you asked. It so much more than just knowing how much money is coming in and going out or how much you have left. It's a well thought out strategy for where your money should go, what it should do **and** the execution of that strategy.

Elder Boyd K. Packer tells this story from his life:

> When I was a boy, we lived in a home surrounded by an orchard. There never seemed to be enough water for the trees. The ditches, always freshly plowed in the spring, would soon fill with weeds. One day, in charge of the irrigation turn, I found myself in trouble. As the water moved down the rows choked with weeds, it would flood in every direction. I worked in the puddles trying to build up the bank. As soon as I had one break patched up, there would be another. A neighbor came through the orchard. He watched for a moment, and then with a few vigorous strokes of the shovel, he cleared the ditch and allowed the water to course through the channel he had made. He said, "If you want the water to stay in its course, you'll have to make a place for it to go." (*Worthy Music, Worthy Thoughts*, 1973 General Conference Address)

Elder Packer used this story to teach us to channel our thoughts, but it can be applied just as well to our money. If you want your money to go to the right places and do the right things you'll have to make a place for it to go. That is what a spending plan does. To create your spending plan, you'll use a basic budget then build it month-by-month and step-by-step into a powerful financial tool.

But before you do any of that there is a **special project** that you must complete. You must establish a **starter emergency fund**. You need a small pile of cash to pay for emergencies, because nothing will derail your financial plan like an unexpected expense or, even worse, a series of them. Murphy's law: "If

> **BIG WORD WARNING**
> A corollary is a statement that naturally follows another statement that is generally accepted as true.

something **can** go wrong, it will." Grandpa's corollary to Murphy's law: "The more prepared you are for an emergency, the less likely it is to happen." And this is never truer than in the world of personal finance.

Establish an emergency fund immediately. Don't save up for it. Don't think about getting around to it. Just do it. Sell your unwanted crap on Facebook Marketplace. Take a temporary part-time job. Hold a carwash for your neighbors. Do whatever it takes to fund your starter emergency fund so you can get on with your spending plan. Young people living at home need $150. A young single adult on their own needs at least $750. Families need a minimum of $1500. Before you do **anything else**, establish this emergency fund.

But Grandpa, I thought you said a pile of cash setting around buys the tools for the devil's workshop. Yes, my grandchild that is true, so having an emergency fund will require some self-control on your part. To make sure this is not one of **those** piles, you are going to do two things.

- **Make it just a little hard to get to.** You want it to be easy enough to get to (after all it's for emergencies), but on the other hand, you should have some time to think before you use it. I recommend a savings or money market account that you can transfer into your checking account. I do not recommend cash under the mattress (too easy to get to) or a CD at the bank (you might have to pay a penalty for early withdrawal).

- **Know what an emergency is.** This is going to be your decision so I suggest you give some serious thought to what an emergency is before you have one. Before you declare an unexpected problem as an emergency, make sure you consider other ways you can **reasonably** solve it. Once you have exhausted those options, ask yourself if the need is necessary and if it is urgent. If it really is an emergency, dip into the emergency fund.

This is not the end of the story when it comes to your emergency fund. Once you use **any** of your emergency money, replace it ASAP. Also, you will eventually want to build your starter emergency fund up to a **major emergency fund**. You will eventually want enough in your fund to cover three to six months of living expenses. To do that, make it part of your regular budgeting process that we are about to discuss.

Okay, back to spending every dollar you ever get through your spending plan.

Step One: Understand your money. Where does it come from? When does it come? How much is coming?

To get to know your money, list all your sources of income and how much is coming from each source in a month. If married, list the income from both spouses. Sometimes you may be able to know exact amounts and other times you may be estimating. If estimating, be conservative. Some expenses like income tax, insurance and savings may already be deducted from your paycheck and that makes budgeting much simpler. If you are an independent contractor or self-employed you will need to budget those expenses yourself. Once you have listed all your after-deduction income sources and amounts add them up.

Your list may look something like this:

His paychecks from job #1	$ 2,000*
His paychecks from job #2	$ 700*
Her paychecks	$ 1,950*
Side Hustle (estimate)	$ 350
Total Take Home	**$ 5,000**

> *It is assumed that taxes and benefits (like health insurance) have already been deducted from these checks, so those items are not reflected here and will not be reflected in the list of expenses below.

Step Two: Understand your expenses. Make a list of all the things you spend money on and estimate how much you spend on each. Then organize them into logical categories. For example, the electric bill, water bill, gas bill would logically be grouped in the "utilities category." Beginning planners often make rookie mistakes (like not budgeting enough) on this step, so give it lots of careful time and thought. Don't just guess; do your research. Your bank and credit card statements and past bills will be good sources for calculating what you have spent in the past and what is coming due.

In organizing your expenses it's important to remember the order of things. God gets paid first (tithing). You get paid second (savings, investment). Everything else get paid third. Because you have a limited about of money left you will need to prioritize. Necessities get paid first and then (and only then) you may buy luxuries.

With help from Dave Ramsey, I suggest this prioritization:

- Four Walls – food, utilities, shelter and transportation.
- Essentials – insurance, debt payments, education, healthcare, childcare, emergency fund and miscellaneous.
- Luxuries – everything else is a luxury. Yes, it's okay to enjoy the luxuries you can afford, but only with money that is left over **and** after you've read "Subsection Six: How do I buy assets instead of liabilities?".

Once you have listed all your expenses for the month add them up.

Your prioritized list might look something like this (based on a $5000 income with deductions already taken out for taxes and insurance):

Tithing	$500
Short-term Savings	$500
Long-term Savings	$500
Investments	$500
Groceries	$500
Utilities	$325
Rent	$1,250
Gasoline	$100
Auto Insurance	$95
Credit Card Payment	$75
Health Savings	$50
Daycare	$800
Emergency Fund	$50
Miscellaneous	$50
Amazon Prime	$15
Date Nights	$50
	$5,360

Step Three: Subtract your expenses from your income and then adjust until you have a zero difference. If your difference is a positive number, Eureka! You have more money to spend, so find a place for it in your plan. If it's a negative number, don't panic. You just need to start making adjustments and keep making adjustments until your difference is zero or.

Using our examples from above, $5000 in income and $5360 in expenses, we have a **negative** difference of $360. We need to make adjustments to bring it to zero. And this where Grandpa's suggestions in the previous section "How do I pay myself second" can be helpful. Let's take a look at those suggestions and see if any of them apply to this situation.

- **Get your pay out of your hands and into savings and investments ASAP.** This suggestion **always** applies, but in this case, it is even more important because money is so tight. I can feel temptation lurking. If your pay-yourself-second money is in your checking or savings account or in cash the devil is already shopping for his tools.

- **Reduce your tax withholding**. This suggestion definitely applies. If you estimate that your withholding is more than your actual tax bill and submit a new W-4, you could make up part of the difference. I don't know if it would make up the whole $360, but it would help make up part. The bad news is that it will take a paycheck or two before the new W-4 is applied to your paycheck, so it may not help with this month.

- **Reduce or defer your actual tax bill**. Timing is even more of an issue with this suggestion.

This is a long-term strategy, but it can make a huge difference in that long-term. It can't help you this month or this year, but can definitely and powerfully help in future years.

- **Reduce your expenses**. This suggestion is **an immediate** solution to this deficit. Grandpa is drooling over all the wonderful ways to cut $360 from this budget. I would immediately zero in on the bottom of the prioritized list of expenses and eliminate my Amazon Prime and Date Night expenses. That's $65 right there and neither of them are necessary to keep you alive or out of jail. Even things higher on the list are good targets for elimination or reduction.

- **Increase your income**. This is **another immediate solution**. Deliver for DoorDash, take a temp job, ask for some overtime at work, sell some of your junk. There are all kinds of temporary fixes to this impending imbalance. Now, you don't want to do this for the rest of your life, so find ways to substantially and permanently increase your income.

- **Play games with your money**. Okay, you're broke this month. Can we turn this into a game and make it fun? Date night can be playing frisbee in the park. Dinner can be frozen veggies in ramen or stone soup. Turn off the lights, turn down the heat and cuddle. See how much you can NOT use your car by walking to school, church or work. And this

> There is a difference between being broke and being poor. Broke is a temporary cash flow problem that you can fix or wait out. Poor is long-term and perpetual with little hope of reversal.

might be the right time to cash in those cans or use some of that skimmed money. Seriously, I have heard dozens of people say that the way they dealt with their broke years were some of their most cherished memories.

- **Ask for help**. Okay, time for a story. When Grandma and Grandpa Bath were young and before we had learned to have a spending plan, we got into a financial bind. I was in college and wanted to go full-time, so I quit my job and we lived off our savings. I did great in school, but we had underestimated our expenses and found that we were running out of money. So, I told Grandma that I was going to quit school, get a job and go back to school at a later time. Bishop Peck called and asked me to come see him. Somehow, he'd found out that we were struggling and that I was going to quit school. He offered to help me through the Church welfare plan. I proudly refused and was ready to walk out of his office when he asked me some questions.

"Do you pay a full tithing?" I replied that I did.

"Do you pay fast offerings?" Yes, I did.

"Have you ever worked on a Church Welfare project?" I told him I had hoed more sugar beets than I cared to remember.

"You have helped others. Let us help you. You have so much to give if you can just get through school."

His kindness and wonderful spirit overcame my pride and I agreed to be helped. He paid our rent for that month and gave us food orders for the next few weeks. It was not easy to take assistance, but within about six weeks I had finished the term with a 4.0 and had found a part-time job as a janitor with the Granite School District. That part-time job led to a full-time job with benefits that fit my school schedule. I worked that job for two and a half years while I finished my degree. If I had not been humbled by the words of that wonderful bishop, I don't know if I'd ever gotten back to school, at least for a long, long time. The point of the story is that if you need help, faithfully ask for it, humbly take it and make the changes you need to become self-reliant. Then when you are self-reliant, help others.

> **BIG WORD WARNING**
> A windfall is an unexpected good fortune, usually having to do with money.

Before leaving the subject of creating a budget, I want to share a special **Grandpa Super Tip** that I've never seen anyone else suggest. That is to create a "next month" expense category. Put away a share of your income into this category each month until it contains enough money to fund your expenses for an entire month. Then use that money to fund your spending plan a month in advance. After that, all the money you make in a month will go into the "next month" category and be there to fund the following month – keeping you a month ahead. Not long after Grandpa and Grandma first started our serious spending plan, a windfall allowed us to fully fund his "next month" category upfront. It has made our financial life much easier and more secure. Remember that piles of cash left lying around buy the devil's tools, so you may want deposit funds for this category in a savings or money market account.

What we have done so far is create a budget, but we don't want a budget. Grandpa doesn't even like the word "budget". So, what must we do to make our budget into a spending plan? The next four steps will turn your budget into a spending plan. Like Great-grandma Bath used to say, "the proof of the pudding is in the eating of it!" A budget starts to become a spending plan when you faithfully execute it and begin "tasting" the benefits.

Step Four: Regularly track your expenses. *At* **least** once a week, you need to sit down with your tracking tools (we'll get to those in a minute) and see where you stand. I say at least once a week, because it doesn't take very long to forget how much you've budgeted and how much you've actually spent. Once a week in good, but more often is better. Some expenses will be easy to track, but others need more diligent supervision.

You need to have tools to track your expenses. When Grandma and I first started we had a spiral-bound notebook, our checkbook and our paper statements that came monthly in the mail. We then graduated to high tech -- an18-column pad and a mechanical pencil. Now we use an Excel spreadsheet and access all of our accounts electronically. Technology has made tracking money so simple that it is foolish not to know where you stand at any given day (or even moment). Start with the tools you have at hand and know how to use; that may just be a notebook and calculator. But I strongly encourage you to learn to use electronic financial tools.

Some of you know how to use Excel better than I do, but if you need a place to begin, go to YouTube and search "google sheets budget template tutorial for beginners." There will be several 10-to-20-minute videos that will lead you step by step through setting up a **basic** Google sheets budget template that you can tweak as you go along. Once you have your tool set up, use it regularly and religiously. **If you are smart, you will look at your tracking tool before you ever spend money**. And that's one of the reasons I suggest the Google sheets budget template. You can download the Google Sheets mobile app onto your phone and manage your budget sheet at any time (e.g. as you're walking into the grocery store).

The first three to four months will be a testing and adjusting period after which, if you are diligent at tracking, you will have a really good handle on your budget. At the end of each month compare your budgeted amount for each category against what you actually spent. If you have a lot of money left over in a category that means you *may* have budgeted too much and need to allocate money to a different category. If you overspend in any category, you either need to budget more money to that category or get a better handle on your spending.

> **Robbing Peter to pay Paul (RPPP) means taking money from one category and giving it to another. This is a slippery slope at best. When you RPPP you tell yourself it's okay to overspend because you can make it up or pay it back later. This is *bad*. Don't do it.**

Adjust your budget at the beginning of each month so that you have a fresh start, with no negative balances and with fully-funded, revised categories. Starting fresh will give you an emotional boost – a do-over. Use that boost to recommit to stay within budget in **all** categories. Adjust your new monthly budget allocations to make up for overspent categories instead of "robbing Peter to pay Paul" (see text box) with flush categories. If you are consistently overspent in one or more catagories, it is time to **seriously** 1) reduce your expenses, 2) increase your income and/or 3) ask for help.

Above all, do not give up on the process. Everybody struggles with the first few months of budgeting and makes rookie mistakes. If you are diligent, you will be surprised how much easier this becomes after a few months. Soon you will have control of your money and will be ready to move on to the next big step.

Step Five: Apply our old friend financial planning to your budget. This means you'll start to strategize, which is the big difference between a budget and a spending plan. Budgeting and tracking your money are good, but a plan is much better. Budgets focus on where you've been and where you are; spending plans focus on where you want to go. Over the three to four months it will take you to master the budging process you'll need to start some serious thinking about where you want your money to go and what you want it to do.

You'll remember that plans are the navigation tools we create to get us where we want to go. Good plans cascade down from a purpose to top-level goals to mid-level goals to lower-level goals and all plans support the goals and purposes above them. So, before you can plan you need to have a purpose.

Some purposes are simple. **I want to know where my money goes. I want to have enough money to get my car fixed when it breaks down. I want to go on a vacation to Disneyland. I want to upgrade to a better car. I want to remodel my house. I want to send my kids to college**. It sounds simple! Earn money, save it up and then spend it. However, just having a bunch of money saved or even invested is not a plan, it's a temptation. A plan is a well-though-out purpose supported by SMART goals that break the mission down into manageable steps.

Take **"taking my kids to Disneyland"** as an example. If going to Disneyland is your WHY, why is it your WHY? *(Oh, come on Grandpa!)* No, seriously! Are you going to Disneyland because you've seen commercials where children shed tears of happiness when they learn they are doing to Disneyland and that is what you want for your kids? (Actually, I'm okay with that if it's what you really, really want!) But could there be other, maybe more important, reasons?

When our kids were little, we took them on all kinds of outings. We went camping, we went on road trips, we went on Church and American history tours. Then, one day, I realized we'd never been to Disneyland, so we bought plane tickets and park passes and went. It was a blast and everyone seemed to have a great time.

The next summer, we took a trip to the Church History site at Martin's Cove, Wyoming. We pulled handcarts from the site over to Independence Rock, camped overnight and then pulled the carts back to Martin's Cove and took the tour. As she was riding in the handcart, little Aunt Hesper (about 6) looked at me and said, "Dad, this is the best vacation we've ever been on."

"Hesper Honey," I replied jokingly, "I took you to Disneyland last year."

She thought for just a moment and then said, "Dad, this is the second-best vacation we've ever been on."

I don't know how the other kids felt, but riding in a bumpy handcart and sleeping in a tent in the wilds of Wyoming were (almost) as much fun as going to Disneyland for my six-year-old. If it was about making her happy or being together on a family adventure, Wyoming worked (almost) as well and cost thousands of dollars less. Don't get me wrong, it's NOT about the money; it's about fulfilling a purpose with a plan.

> I am not telling you how to run your family – that's up to you. This is not a book on family relations, it is a book on money. If, after careful consideration, your family financial plan includes a trip to Disneyland, say hello to Mickey for me. But make sure it is part of your plan.

What I am saying is that our trip to Disneyland was not an important part of a well-thought-out plan, supporting the well-thought-out purpose of family togetherness. It was just a fun and impulsive whim that cost a chunk of change.

Is there anything wrong with that? Well, no and yes! **No!** We had the money in the bank and paid cash for the trip. We had a great time as a family. We made family memories. Disneyland was a fun, wholesome place. Spending money is not bad. Being spontaneous is fun. But also, **Yes!** Because it was not part of our spending plan. And why not? Because we didn't have a spending plan. We just had a pile of money in the bank and when the idea of going to Disneyland crossed my mind, I had no other plans for that money, so "why not?" Could the money have been better spent to fulfill our family purposes – financial or otherwise? I can think back to a dozen or so financial situations in our family that could have been **significantly** improved if we had formulated a plan early on. Let me give you just one example.

Our family has always driven "beater" cars. Okay, maybe not beater cars, but it sure felt like it. This is partly because I am not a big car guy, but it is mostly because we didn't have a financial plan that included car repair and replacement.

Determined to never have a car payment, I would drive our cars until the "wheels fell off" and then buy whatever I could afford to pay cash for. Our cars were often in need of repairs and that was often an emergency because I had not saved enough money for car repairs. A couple of times while we were on trips, our family car broke down and we were stranded. It was seldom dangerous, but always frustrating, embarrassing and an added expense. When each of these "emergencies" happened, I would RPPP and we would have to go without something else we wanted or needed.

We weren't horrible financial stewards. We lived within our means. We saved for retirement. The only debt we ever had was our modest home mortgage. So why did we drive fifteen-year-old vans rather than two-year-old Suburbans? Why were we always scrambling to pay for car repairs? Why did we never get ahead in the car game? It would have been nice if we'd had a big bucket of money labeled "New Car" or "Car Repairs" when we needed it.

Yeah, Grandpa, that would be a great idea. If you like that idea, we'll come back to it in just a few minutes, but for now, let's get back to our question about getting ahead in the car game? What if you designed a spending plan to provide nicer cars for your family. It might look something like this:

The purpose: "Providing a quality lifestyle for our family."

Top-level goal: "Provide safe, reliable and comfortable transportation."

Mid-level goals: "Save $2400 a year towards a new car purchase" and "Maintain a $1000 car repair fund."

Low-level goals (under the "new car" mid-level goal : "Budget $200 a month to the new car fund" and "Contribute $200 in an interest-earning CD each month." This would be an ongoing, standing goal. When the time was right, we would have had cash to upgrade our car. Every dollar given a job and being there to do it.

> **BIG WORD WARNING**
> **Serendipitous means discovered by chance in a happy or beneficial way – like birthday cash from Grandpa.**

Could one of our top-level goals, supporting the purpose: "Create a healthy family culture", be "Take a family vacation to Disneyland"? Without a doubt! And part of that plan could be to fund a CD for that trip. The money could come from your regular income, the kids' dog poop scooping business, yard sale proceeds, or any number of planned (or even serendipitous) sources. This would most likely be a short-term goal and once accomplished, the money going toward this goal could go to funding a new goal.

These plans could have been part of the spending plan encompassing all of our money. No money left in piles to tempt us. Every dollar assigned to a well-planned-out purpose. Some of the money would have been in our checking account to cover regular monthly expenditures – mortgage, groceries, gas, utilities, etc. Some of the money would be in money market accounts to cover medium-term or unscheduled expenditures like emergencies. Some of it would be in interest bearing certificates of deposit (CDs) for short-term and long-term

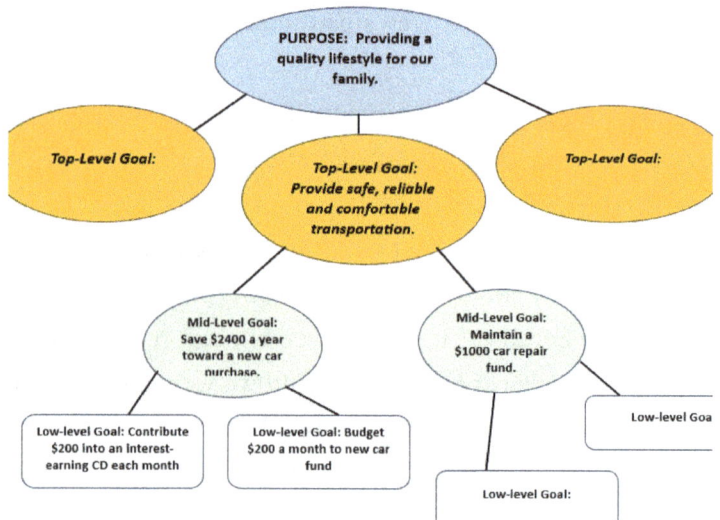

saving goals, generally the kind that are anticipatable or schedulable. Some of it would be in mutual funds earning towards the future.

Grandpa, do you really expect me to go to all that work and plan out my finances so that every single dollar is accounted for and has a job and a place to go to wait for that job? **Emphatically, yes!** The alternatives are to stumble through your financial life blindly, or to do the job half-way and be somewhat successful if you're lucky.

But if you still like that idea of big buckets of money, I have good news. You have already started creating them as part of your spending plan. Magic buckets of money can be there when you need them. I am deadly serious here! Read on!

Step Six: Create magic buckets of money. These magic buckets only appear when you use the **magic words** and **wave the magic wand**. The money that is in them is alive, awake and growing. It is also smart and loyal – never losing its way or shirking its duty.

These buckets appear when you create them as part of your spending plan. They will show up in your financial goals, budget, tracking tools, bank and investment accounts. The **magic words are,** "As part of this goal we will create a bucket of money called…" Your **budget and tracking tool become magic wands** when you create and assign money to categories. The magic buckets are **special accounts** and when you actually put money in them, that money comes alive, wakes up, grows and loyally waits there to do its job.

Setting up special accounts is not difficult to do, but it does require effort and organization on your part. You will need to use a bank or credit union that allows you to set up multiple CD's and sub-accounts within your account. You may also need the help of an investment brokerage, but we will talk more about that in our sub-section on waking up your money and putting it to work.

Your **first bucket is your checking account**. It serves as the place to park the money you will use in the most immediate future (the next month or two). We're talking about expenses like tithing, rent, utilities, groceries, gas, and any money you have been saving but are now

> **BIG WORD WARNNG**
> **Liquidity is the ability to convert assets into cash quickly without incurring a loss in value.**

ready to spend. You will probably not earn any interest on this money, which is the tradeoff for having total liquidity.

Your **next buckets will be saving accounts and money market accounts** for your emergency fund and some short-term savings. You'll be earning a little interest while you wait to use it and it can be easily liquidated as needed.

Your **next buckets will be higher interest-earning accounts** like certificates of deposit (CDs) for most of your savings. CDs incur a penalty for early withdrawal, so you **don't** want to use them for money you plan to spend soon, but they are great for money you are saving up. In addition, a growth CD will allow you to continue to contribute to that CD so your money grows through both interest accumulation and contribution.

A magic bucket for redecorating your family room in two years would be a perfect example of a growth CD bucket. If your spending plan calls for you save $200 a month. You establish a 6-month growth CD with your first $200 deposit and it immediately begins earning 4.25%. Each month you reinvest the interest and add $200. In six months, when the CD matures you will not only have your $1200, but a bonus of over 10 bucks. Repeat the process for the next 18 months and when you are ready to decorate, you will have over $5000 at your disposal.

Once you have established such accounts, every dollar will have a name, a place and a job. It will be alive and growing, ready to serve you when the time comes. The dashboard of your online banking account might look something like the chart to the right.

No Fee Checking 2500-001	$3822.25
Savings One – Auto Repairs 2500-002	$ 359.00
Savings Two – Disneyland 2500-003	$ 120.25
Savings Three – Remodel 2500-004	$ 395.60
Savings Four – Tuition 2500-005	$ 221.00
Money Market – Emergency 2500-0060	$6000.00
6 Month CD – New Car 2500-0020	$2195.00
6 Month CD – Down Payment 2500-0021	$4195.50

You may not be as impressed with this as Grandpa seems to be. After all, these are not huge numbers we are dealing with here. And it may sound like a hassle to establish special savings accounts and CDs. If you are feeling this way, the following paragraph is for you. It's obvious that you've not paid enough tuition to my old alma mater, The School of Hard Knocks. What a dilemma! The most powerful lessons in finance are often best taught by disappointment and failure at old SHK, but here is Grandpa trying to teach them to you the easy way – vicariously.

Trust Grandpa! The feelings of peace and confidence that come from having a financial plan and control of your finances is worth much more than the thrills that come from having or spending a bunch of money. Grandpa's even better news is that with your last set of magic buckets you can have both peace and a bunch of money to spend.

The last, and most magical, buckets are the investments you can make to grow wealth. Most of these magic buckets will not be in your bank account, but in stocks, bonds, mutual funds, real estate, commodities, loans, partnerships and businesses. We will talk more about the logistics of these in our sub-section on waking up your money and putting it to work. For now, consider these points.

- In America, you blessed little sweethearts, magic investment buckets are not just reserved for the rich or their children.

- These magic investment buckets start to fill as soon as you start paying yourself second.

- The more generously and more consistently you allocate money to your investment magic buckets, the easier and surer it is that you will create wealth and you can create a lot of it.

- Investment magic buckets are long-term strategies. Any plan to get rich quick is suspicious at best and can be very dangerous. Patience is your friend.

- Although a plethora of options exist for investment, the best thing for most people to do is start with affordable, time-tested and proven strategies – like mutual funds. You can grow and diversify into other investments as you learn and grow.

BIG WORD WARNNG
A plethora is a large or excessive amount of something.

Step Seven: Get on with your life. This is a funny thing to say after pages and pages of focusing on accumulating and managing money, but it is a very important last step. All of our financial thinking, planning and executing is designed to give us peace and freedom, to allow us to live a good life without worrying about (**or** lusting for **or** obsessing over) money.

Remember the story of the farrier and rich rancher. As long as the farrier could hear the pennies dropping into the bucket, or even the rancher calling out the numbers, he was miserable. He finally told the rancher to just let him concentrate on doing a good job and let the money take care of itself.

That is what I am asking you to do. Build the foundation of self-reliance and independence. Learn the proper attitudes toward money. Do your planning. Get a good education and learn to work. Manage your money properly. Then get on with life!

Chapter 6: How Do I Do What's Simple but Not Easy?

I have decided to group the next three subsections together in their own chapter because they have two powerfully common themes.

1. These are the "higher" aspects of personal finance; things the huge majority of people don't do. And because they don't do them, they are trapped in the earn-and-spend cycle that Robert Kiyosaki calls the rat race. I was once asked to volunteer at my kids' high school in a program called Reality Town. It was designed to help students learn how to handle their money. It was not a bad program; it taught students that some careers pay better than others, the basics of budgeting and that every aspect of a chosen lifestyle comes at a price, but it **did not** teach the students the difference between assets and liabilities, the power of investment or the danger of debt. I don't think the people who designed the program wanted the students stuck in the cycle, but they may not have understood (or thought the students could understand) these higher aspects. Grandpa, on the other hand believes that my grandchildren are smart enough to understand them. I will teach them to you and hope you are wise enough to apply them.

2. The principles of each of these subsections can be simply stated in a sentence or two, but they are not that easy to master. For example, I could simply say, "Debt bad, cash good!" and leave it at that, but I guarantee that most of the people who believe that mantra find themselves taking on debt and regretting it. And believe me, it's so very, very easy to get into debt and so very difficult to live debt free. But it can be done and I will teach you how to do it.

So, let's begin looking at the three higher aspects of personal finance.

Subsection Four: How do I avoid debt like the plague?

Before you read this subsection, I want you to Google "SNL don't buy stuff" and take three minutes to watch the Saturday Night Live skit that comes up in the search. When you've done that, you will understand THE MAJOR POINT. Avoiding debt is really simple, just pay cash for everything and you will have no debt. It's that simple, but not that easy.

I guarantee you will be **sorely** tempted to borrow money tens of thousands of times in your life. I will be very surprised and proud of you if you never do. The purpose of this subsection is to outline a strategy for HOW you can be the weirdest person among your group of friends – the one that pays cash for everything and only buys what you can afford.

And that brings us to a very important point about debt. There is **no good debt**, but there are rare occasions where debt may be **acceptable**. Acceptable forms of debt must be used sparingly and retired as quickly as possible. I am hesitant to list examples of acceptable debt, because I don't want to be the one to give you an excuse for borrowing money. I will, however, talk about a few later in this subsection. If you are diligent in handling your money, apply the principles I am about to teach you and seek the guidance of the Holy Ghost, you will know when incurring a debt is right for you and acceptable to the Lord.

So, here are my suggestions for HOW to avoid debt.

1. Use the power of cash

The phrase "cash is king" has been around since at least the 1890s and comes back into vogue whenever the power of having and using cash is demonstrated. Dave Ramsey uses the phrase in the intro to his radio show and he uses it to refer to the power that cash has over debt in personal finance. In general, the term "cash" refers to the money you actually have on hand or in your bank account(s).

While using **hard cash**, meaning bills and coins you can hold in your hand, has power (we'll talk about that in a minute), there can be some cons. Security is an issue; if you lose it, it's gone. Record keeping can be a hassle. It can be inconvenient to carry large amounts of cash or even remember to keep cash in your pocket. And not all establishments accept cash as payment.

However, most of these problems can be solved with the use of a debit card, which is essentially like using cash. A debit card looks like a credit card and can be used like a credit card, but the money comes out of your bank account electronically as soon as you swipe it. It's more secure than actual cash; can be canceled and replaced if stolen and gives you a record of your purchases. You can use it to access large amounts of cash

> Personal cheques are another alternative to hard cash but they are not used much for everyday expenses. They are not very secure and a lot of places just won't take them anymore.

without carrying a wad of bills around and it's accepted almost anywhere. It's very convenient, but must be safeguarded just like hard cash and may not be quite as powerful as hard cash.

There are some things you **don't** want to do with cash. Don't have an overdraft on your bank account; this encourages overspending and costs you fees. Limit your use of ATMs, especially if you're using ATMs that charge you fees. With those logistics aside, let's talk about the power of cash and what it can do for you?

- **Cash creates a natural barrier to overspending**. If you use cash exclusively, you can only spend the money you have in your pocket or in your account. If you go to the grocery store and fill your cart with $100 with of groceries, but only have $75, you will have to put back the big bag of M&Ms, buy the smaller bottle of catsup and swap brand name products for store brands. It might be a little embarrassing at checkout, but that will only happen once before you learn.

- **Hard cash keeps your personal business more private and confidential.** Although you may never be totally free from financial surveillance, whenever you use hard cash, your electronic footprint is greatly reduced. It will be harder for others to know what you bought or what you paid for it. You'll be far less likely to receive annoying little ads on your Facebook feed based on your spending habits. Note that using a debit card will subject you to some of the same invasions into your business as with a credit card.

- **Using cash hurts a little but helps you stay on budget**. Money has undeniable psychological power, which has been (and continues to be) confirmed through scientific research. One of the things we know about using hard cash is that it activates pain centers in your brain when you hand it over to someone else. This emotional pain discourages spending and makes you more likely to look for bargains – helping you to stay on budget. The effect is greatly lessened when you use a debit card.

Here is the citation for one scientific study on the pain of handing over money. *Mazar, Nina and Plassmann, Hilke and Robitaille, Nicole and Lindner, Axel, Pain of Paying? — A Metaphor Gone Literal: Evidence from Neural and Behavioral Science (December 16, 2016). Rotman School of Management Working Paper No. 2901808, INSEAD Working Paper No. 2017/06/MKT,* Available at SSRN: **https://ssrn.com/abstract=2901808 or http://dx.doi.org/10.2139/ssrn.2901808**

- **Cash can give you bargaining power and a psychological advantage.** Some other scientific studies of the psychological power of money suggest that money affects our brains much like cocaine; and that counting money can actually relieve pain and make us feel stronger. Now, put those three ideas together as we negotiate the price of a used car from a private seller. He wants $12,000, but we think $10,000 is a fairer price. What do you think goes on in his

Here is an article that summarizes the studies I used in this bullet point: Steve Gillman, *Scientists Figured Out How Money Affects Your Brain and It's Fascinating*, April 18, 2016, Available at: **https://www.thepennyhoarder.com/make-money/side-gigs/psychology-of-money/**

head if he watches you pull a hundred $100 bills from your pocket and count them out to him (or, better yet, let him count them)? Science suggests you'll most likely have a deal and he will feel really good as he signs the title over. This might be less likely to happen if you offer him a check, and even less likely if you offer to go to the bank and get a loan. (By the way, another study suggests that he may be even less likely to strike a deal with you if you really lowball him, so don't try ripping people off, just get a fair deal.)

- **Cash finalizes the deal.** Once you have paid cash, the financial part of the transaction is done.

There are no fees. There is no interest. There is no debt. Now, wisdom dictates that you have a clear and mutual agreement before any money changes hands and for bigger ticket items, written documentation – like a bill of sale or executed contract. And you will **always** want a detailed receipt.

2. Understand what debt really is.

The alternative to cash is debt (often called credit) and it has become the preferred method of commerce. Most adults carry at least one credit card in their wallet and some use it for almost everything they buy. For larger purchases you can use loans – car loans, home improvement loans, personal loans, payday and title loans. It is so very, very easy to use credit and it is highly encouraged. Whole industries make their money by getting people to borrow.

I won't spend a lot of time on the dangers of debt because I have already covered that in our WHY section. Instead, I will spend some time on **some definitions and explanations** that will help you see how debt works.

- **Debt is borrowing money or otherwise obligating yourself** to pay money in the future. That makes credit card charges, mortgages, car loans, phone contracts, subscription services, pawning your stuff, student loans, payday loans, title loans, personal loans, IOUs, medical bills and unpaid taxes all debt. If you are obligated to pay any amount to anybody, you are in debt.

> **Pawning is when you take something you own to a pawn shop and they lend you money on it. If you don't pay off the loan within a certain time, they sell what you've pawned.**

- **Credit is your reputation**. Credit is often used to determine if you can borrow money and how much you have to pay in interest and fees. The most common way of measuring your credit is with a **credit score** issued by a credit reporting agency. If you follow my advice, you will only be borrowing money on rare occasions (if at all) and your **credit score** may not be too high. This may make it difficult in those rare occasions when you do need to borrow money (like getting a mortgage) and, unfortunately, landlords, insurance companies, employers and others often use your credit score to determine if you are the kind of person they want to do business with. So, what can you do? Here are some suggestions:
  - o Use service providers that report your utility, rent, cell phone and insurance payments to credit bureaus to improve your credit score.
  - o If you are taking out a mortgage, ask for a lender that uses **manual** underwriting and have a big down payment to grease the wheels.
  - o Keep meticulous records of your payment history and present it in lieu of a credit score.
  - o Learn to sell your debt-free lifestyle as a desirable quality and evidence of trustworthiness.

- **Fees are a sneaky way to make more money off of you.** Fees are a way of financial life. Some are levied to discourage poor behavior, others buy exclusivity, but many times fees are just designed to hide costs or make a little extra money off of the unwary. And this last use is never more prevalent than in the world of debt. Grandpa has compiled a list of fees in Appendix B for you to consider. It's not a total list of fees, but it gives you the idea. When you borrow, you are often "nickel-and-dimed" out of a lot more of your hard-earned money than you expect.

- **Interest is the biggest fee of all.** On top of all the little fees you can be charged is the mother of all fees – interest. Interest can be as high as 600%. (*I am not making this up **nor** talking about loan sharks who send Guido to break your knee caps if you don't pay up. These are actual rates from "payday" lending institutions.*) Interest rates depend on the type of loan, the security you put up, the price of money and the profit the lender wants to make. I have also included a sampling of different types of loans and their terms in Appendix B. Check it out. One last thing to say about interest is that it never sleeps. It starts the minute you incur the debt and keeps adding up until the debt is paid in full.

- **The devil is in the details.** The interest **rate** is not the whole story when it comes to a loan. Among the many other variables that determine how much borrowing is going to cost are the length of the loan, the payment terms, and whether it is simple interest or compound interest.
  - The **term of the loan** is how long it takes to pay it off. Until that day, you will be paying interest. A longer term equals lower payments, but more interest. A shorter term means a higher payment, but less interest.
  - **Payment terms** are the rules for paying the money back. Most loans require a **minimum** monthly payment that covers the interest for that month and something on the principal (amount still owing on the loan). However, some minimum loan payments only cover the interest or **part** of the interest. **Or** lenders will be really "nice" and let you skip a payment or two. In these cases, the unpaid interest is added to your principal so you're paying interest on interest. Minimum or skipped payments can keep you in debt forever, paying tons of interest. On the other hand, **if** your payment terms allow you to make additional principal payments, you can get out of debt faster and pay less in interest.
  - There is a **difference between simple and compound-interest** loans. With a **simple-interest loan**, you only pay interest on what's left of the original principal. With a **compound-interest loan**, you pay interest on the balance owned, plus any additional interest that is owed. If you don't make at least a full-interest payment **or** are allowed to skip payments, the lender isn't worried because he'll just add the unpaid interest to the principal and charge you interest on both. Oh, and by the way, the interest in **now not compounding monthly, it's happening daily**. Sound like a scam? Yes, it's called credit card and student loan debt and the reason why some people are caught in a lifetime of debt.

3. Remove temptation

You may think that just learning about the dangers of debt has scared any thought of borrowing from your mind and you will never be tempted. I hope so, but experience has shown that debt is very, very seductive. For that reason, it is very important that you remove the temptation to borrow from your life.

One way to do this is to eliminate debt-producing instruments from your reach. Cut up your credit cards. Cancel your overdraft protection. Get rid of your personal and home equity lines of credit. Delete any credit card information you may have on shopping apps. Immediately shred any credit card offers than come in the mail. Cancel any auto-pay memberships or subscriptions you may have. The harder it is for you to borrow money, the less likely you will be to do it.

Train yourself and your family to use cash. This may be a difficult transition for a couple of reasons. One, is that cash is harder to track, so you must have a system for doing that. Using a debit card will help, but for some people a debit card is too much like a credit card and they may need to resort to hard cash until their brain adjusts. Two, is that it will require you to think through your finances more carefully and in advance. In the long run, you'll be grateful you became a better planner and more intentional actor, but at first it may drive you a little crazy.

Further remove temptation by following the 24-hour rule, which is to wait **at least** 24 hours before making an unplanned purchase or obligation. I discussed earlier how counting money can give you a high, well it turns out that spending money can do something similar – it can release dopamine (a neurotransmitter associated with reward or pleasure) into your system. This can cause you to impulse spend (especially if you are stressed or bored); give into peer pressure (let's go catch a movie tonight); or make rash decisions (based on limited information). The 24-hour rule brings you back to mindfulness, forcing delayed gratification and giving your brain time to enjoy the thought of spending and then come back to your senses. The 24-hour rule also serves as a great excuse. When you are feeling pressured into doing something you can't afford or don't want to do, just say, "I have this hard fast rule…" It's important to remember that the rule states, "**at least 24-hours**." For bigger expenditures or more serious obligations, I suggest more time – a week, a month, a year. Enjoy the dopamine rush by thinking about spending the money and then take your time coming back to mindfulness.

4. Establish realistic expectations

One of the major causes of people going into debt is that they're trying to meet unrealistic expectations. Expectations are pictures we paint in our minds of the way things ought to be. They become filters through which we judge our lives and when our lives don't match the picture, we may choose to sink into despair, or do whatever we think we need to make our lives match our expectations. One of the things we may do is borrow money.

For example, you see on social media that some of your friends are taking cruises and you create in your mind an expectation that you need to take a cruise. That's okay if it's what you really, really want and you plan for it; save for it; shop for it and pay cash for it, but if you just feel like a loser because you're the "only person in the world" not taking a cruise, you just created an unrealistic expectation. It's now much easier to be seduced into debt to take a cruise.

Please understand! Grandpa thinks high expectations (and nice vacations) are good. They motivate us to work hard so we can do better and enrich our lives. What I am warning about are **unrealistic** expectations – expectations that are too high or that flow from bad or false premises.

Let's go back to our cruise example. Who says taking a cruise it the right thing to do? Did that come from a long, heartfelt desire; a prompting from the Spirit; or a recommendation from your doctor? Or did it come from your friends' Instagram posts, flashy and sexy brochures in the mail, or a fear of missing out? And what makes a cruise the right move at this time in your life? Can you afford it or will you have to borrow money to make it happen? And even if you pay cash for it, will taking this cruise delay or derail some other important goals?

One day, Alma, the Younger realized he was having unreal expectations and that he needed to adjust his thinking. Here is his unrealistic expectation from Alma 29:

> O that I were an angel, and could have the wish of mine heart, that I might go forth and speak with the trump of God, with a voice to shake the earth, and cry repentance unto every people!
>
> Yea, I would declare unto every soul, as with the voice of thunder, repentance and the plan of redemption, that they should repent and come unto our God, that there might not be more sorrow upon all the face of the earth. (Alma 29:1-2)

Talk about righteous desires! This guy doesn't want to cruise the Mexican Riviera, he wants to be a powerful, gospel-proclaiming angel. Can't get any better than that, right? WRONG! Listen to what he says next.

> But behold, I am a man, and **do sin in my wish**; for **I ought to be content** with the things which the Lord hath allotted unto me. (Emphasis added)
> (Alma 29:3)

How did this happen to a prophet? I don't know for sure, but I have a good idea. Alma had just met up with the Sons of Mosiah, who had pulled off one of the most miraculous missionary journeys in history. And they were bringing their strongest converts home with them. Alma had been stuck in Zarahemla, trying to keep apostasy and evil at bay – not the most exciting work. Now, the Lamanites had attacked and killed hordes of his people. If I were Alma, I'd be fantasizing about being a powerful, earth-shaking, thundering angel too, but it wasn't the right thing or the right time – it was unrealistic.

How can we know if our expectations are realistic? Realistic expectations flow from down-to-earth, intentional and spiritual sources. They are well thought out. They have a purpose and an achievable path to fulfillment. The thoughts of realistic expectations may not thrill you like the fantasy of unrealistic expectations, but they will be satisfying and fill you with joy. It's okay to dream and dream big, but you must dream realistically. Under these guidelines, "I'm going to live in a mansion!" becomes "I'm going to live in a comfortable home that meets my needs." "I gotta have that new I-phone!" becomes "I will upgrade my phone when this one quits working." "I'll play the lotto and get rich!" becomes "I will save and invest my money to get rich."

Before we leave the subject of expectations, I want to say a few things about the false expectation that all your dreams will come true, if you just want them badly enough. With all deference to my fellow Granite High alumni, Leigh Harline, who helped write the unofficial Disney theme song, **When You Wish Upon a Star,** I have to say "What a crock!" Dreams do not come true just because we wish them. Some requests can be too extreme. Fate is not necessarily your friend and will not always step in and make it all okay.

Realistic dreams require a path, a plan, dedication, hard work, time and the grace of a loving God. There will be times when you stumble and fall; get off course, slack off, get impatient, waste time, pay the stupid tax and even sin. There will be limitations, roadblocks, storms and hardships. You may not make your first million by the time you are 30, or 40, or 50 or ever.

And our financial dreams don't come true just because we are righteous. It's been said, "Want to hear God laugh? Share your life plan with Him." But if you are a true and faithful servant, God will lead you through the minefields of life and support you in your trials as he takes you where He wants you to go and has you do what He wants you to do. And you will be happy about it. I love this C.S. Lewis quote below.

> **"Imagine yourself as a living house. God comes in to rebuild that house. At first, perhaps, you can understand what He is doing. He is getting the drains right and stopping the leaks in the roof and so on; you knew that those jobs needed doing and so you are not surprised. But presently He starts knocking the house about in a way that hurts abominably and does not seem to make any sense. What on earth is He up to? The explanation is that He is building quite a different house from the one you thought of - throwing out a new wing here, putting on an extra floor there, running up towers, making courtyards. You thought you were being made into a decent little cottage: but He is building a palace. He intends to come and live in it Himself." C.S. Lewis, *Mere Christianity***

5. Be a great shopper

Your Great-Uncle Zane Gray (the welder, not the author) was a great shopper. Once I was having a conversation with his wife, Great-Aunt Jacky and she expressed how glad she was that he'd finally bought a truck. I asked her what she meant by "finally" and she explained.

Apparently, it had taken him quite a while to buy that truck. He had researched the make, model, and features he wanted. He did more research to determine what an excellent price would be. Then he started shopping. He shopped and shopped and shopped. When he finally found the right truck, at the right price, (two years later) he plopped down the money and took it home.

I told Jacky that I was impressed that he was so careful about buying that truck. She responded with a sigh, "He does that with everything." I watched and it was true. He was a great shopper. And I have come to understand that one of the most powerful ways of avoiding debt is to be a great shopper. Let me outline what I mean.

1. **A great shopper is patient**. Part of what made Uncle Zane's truck purchase so impressive, is that he waited until he found exactly what he wanted at the right price. If you can cultivate this kind of patience, you'll be far less tempted to impulse buy, pay too much, be unhappy with your purchase or spend money you shouldn't.

Shopping online can be both friend and foe in developing this skill. Imagine that you go to local stores to find something and they don't have exactly what you want; then go home and find it online. It you are normal, you're so excited to find it, you throw it into your cart, charge it on your credit card and Amazon will have it to you the next day. If you're abnormal (and we want to be abnormal), you will make a note of your research and continue your search. Oh, you'll get remarketing ads on your social media feeds, but you'll ignore them until you determine a great price for that item. You can use one of several apps that help track the price. When it goes on sale for your price, you can snatch it up, if you still want or need it.

Did you see the pros and cons of online shopping in this example? Online shopping helped you find just what you were looking for, shop several different sources, determine a good price and track the price until it came down to your ideal. On the other hand, shopping online made it so tempting and easy to buy now, you were enticed by retargeting ads that popped up after your initial research and what the heck, free shipping.

It takes focus and determination to be a patient shopper.

2. **A great shopper gets at least three bids.** How do you know if you are getting a good price? You let the free market decide. Way back in 1776, Scottish economist Adam Smith wrote about the "invisible hand" that fairly regulates free markets. It is a combination of self-interest and competition. You can take advantage of this invisible hand when you shop, if you 1) look out for your own interests and 2) use competition to get a good deal.

Let's suppose you get your annual springtime air conditioner check. Afterward, the tech tells you your unit is still working, but getting really old and should be replaced before the summer starts. He makes a good sales pitch (outlawed freon, inflation, possible damage to your furnace) and gives you a $13,000 bid. What do you do?

One of the most important tactics you can use is to make him compete. If you thank him for his bid and let him know you will be asking at least two of his competitors to bid the same job, he will start to rethink his offer. As a matter of fact, if he amends it right then, you know that competition is pretty stiff in the HVAC business. Even if he gives you a better price, follow through and have other companies come in and bid the job.

As you get these bids, pay attention and take careful notes. Ask plenty of questions and don't be afraid to share and compare competitors' offers. Make sure you are comparing like equipment, labor and service – "apples to apples" as they say. If you pay attention, you can learn a lot about products and services offered by the different companies and be able to better speak their language.

Remember that you are concerned about your own self interests. Don't feel badly about discussing, or even challenging, the details of a bid. Tell them what the other contractors are willing to do for you. Don't be influenced by how nice the salesperson is – they are paid to be nice and build relationships of trust. Always check the companies' credentials and ratings. And a bid is no good unless you have it in writing. I will warn you that this will not make you popular. Businesses may not like it when you comparison shop.

But good shoppers will do this with everything they possibly can. Now, you may not be in the mood to discuss prices or get additional bids when you are lying in the emergency room, needing an emergency gall bladder operation, but if you are in the dentist chair discussing a non-emergency procedure, that's great time to discuss getting some other bids.

3. **A great shopper let's endorphins run their course.** As discussed earlier, having a hard fast rule to wait **at least** 24 hours before making a purchase allows the new-purchase endorphins to run their course. Good shoppers use this strategy often and will extend it. Often, if you wait long enough, you'll decide you really don't want or need that thing that was so exciting a little while ago and you'd rather use your money for something else.

Back to our new air conditioner example, could you go ahead and get the bids, know which company will most likely give you the best deal and then wait for your old air condition to quit? (That may actually take a couple of summers.) Or what if it does quit and you live without air conditioning for one summer – like people did for thousands of years before air conditioners were invented – and then get the buy-an-air-conditioner-and-get-a-free-furnace deal during the winter? A really good shopper would!

4. **A great shopper uses cash.** You probably are now seeing how interrelated all of these principles are. A good shopper understands the phycological power of cash – both in getting the deal and helping you as a consumer feel good about your purchases. Using cash helps you be patient, look for the best deal, be realistic in your expectations and fight the temptation to overspend. Using cash and avoiding debt should not just be a good financial strategy, it should become a way of life.

5. Eliminate your debt

I have been writing this section on avoiding debt as if I caught you before you incurred any. However, there is a good chance, that you are already in debt or that you may incur debt in the future. If that is the case, don't feel too badly, it happens and it can be fixed.

Before we talk about eliminating debt, let's return to our discussion about times when incurring debt may be appropriate. If you or a member of your family gets cancer or needs heart bypass surgery, it would be foolish to refuse treatment because you haven't saved up the money for chemotherapy or an operation. If you are in an otherwise healthy financial situation, you may decide to buy a house and it can take a long time to save up cash for even a modest one. If your calling in life is to be a medical doctor, it may be difficult to go to medical school without some financial help – maybe from loans. You will ultimately be the judge of when debt is appropriate for you. Just remember that if you *need* to incur debt, the best counsel is to borrow as little as possible; enter into the loan with your eyes wide open and then pay it off as quickly as you can. That is all I am going to say about acceptable debt.

Here's how to eliminate debt!

Establish a solid, basic financial foundation. Pay a fair and honest tithing, establish a starter emergency fund, and establish a frugal, balanced spending plan that includes at least the minimum payment for each debt. By the way, the more you can cut expenses and the more you can increase your income, the more you can throw at your debt.

Except for employer-sponsored 401K contributions, temporarily suspend paying yourself second. Debt is dangerous and can ruin your life. Eliminating it must be high priority and you have to throw everything at it. Employer-sponsored 401K contributions are the exception to the rule for two reasons. 1) Your employer is most likely matching part of your contribution and that is free money. 2) You employer may be paying the management fees associated with your investment accounts and that is free money. Don't take money out of your retirement fund to pay debt. You **never** want to break the positive cycle of investing, earning, compounding and earning.

List all of your debts and the minimum payment needed to service each debt. Make sure your minimum payments cover, at least, the monthly interest or you will be paying compound interest and losing ground. **Exclude** your home mortgage from this list, but **include** your home equity lines of credit (HELOCs).

Attack your debt using either the debt avalanche or the debt snowball.

The **debt avalanche** means that you throw all of the money you would be paying yourself second, all of the money you can cut out of your budget, all the extra money you can earn, all of your financial windfalls and the kitchen sink at the loan with the **highest interest rate**. You keep pounding at that loan until it is paid off. Then you take all of the money you have been paying on that loan and apply it to the loan with the second highest interest rate. Keep pounding at that loan until it is paid off. Then you take all of the money you have been paying on the first two loans and apply them to the loan with next highest rate. Repeat until they are all gone.

The **debt snowball** is the same as the debt avalanche in that you throw everything at it. The difference is that you attack the loan with the **lowest balance** first, second lowest balance second and so on until they are all paid off.

The advantage to the avalanche method is that you save more money in interest and it may work faster. It works best if you have large higher-interest debts (like credit cards) and if you are naturally self-motivated. The snowball method gives you quick wins which are very motivating. It is also easier to implement. It works best if the interest rates on your loans are pretty similar or if you need that emotional boost to keep going.

When you've paid all your debts, except for your mortgage, return to normalcy in your budget.

Restart paying yourself second and work to fully fund your emergency fund (3-6 months of expenses). After you have fully funded your emergency fund and made good headway purchasing some wealth building assets, consider attacking your mortgage debt.

I am a huge fan of paying off your mortgage. If you own your home free and clear, except for property taxes, casualty insurance and maintenance you will never have to pay for a place to live. You will have ultimate housing security. Your home will most likely appreciate in value, helping to make you wealthy. You could take the money formerly used to service your mortgage, invest it and become wealthy even faster.

However, paying off your mortgage needs to be a matter of balance. If all of your wealth is tied up in your home, the only way you'll be able to access it is to sell your home or borrow against it. Your plan to pay off your mortgage should not prevent you from buying other income-generating assets or you could end up "house poor." In addition, you can sometimes earn significantly more in a simple and safe investment than you're paying in interest on your mortgage. If this is the case you may want to invest your extra money rather than pay down the mortgage.

Having said all of that, I believe that all good financial plans include mortgage payoff acceleration (regularly making extra principal payments). Being in a strong equity position (owing a lot less than your house is worth) is a safeguard against hard times and will give you security and confidence. Your challenge will be to find the right balance between paying down your mortgage and investing for wealth.

Subsection Five: How do I put my money to work?

When Uncle VJ was about five years old, he asked me, "Where in the scriptures does it say you can't be rich?"

My answer to him was, "Nowhere! As a matter of fact, the Book of Mormon says that if you seek the kingdom of God first, it's okay to seek riches if you will use them for the right reasons." (see Jacob 2:18-19)

End of discussion, right? No way! He then turned to me and asked, "Then how come you're not rich!?"

Ouch! How was I to explain to a five-year-old why I was not rich. The answer I gave him was not totally honest. It was a smokescreen covering up embarrassment. My son could tell I was way more like George Bailey than Scrouge McDuck.

Forty years later, I sit at my computer imagining you asking, *"Grandpa, since you are about to tell me how to get wealthy, are you wealthy?"* I know you are too polite to ask that question, but, if you are going to give any credence to my advice, it needs to be asked and answered. And my answer is Yes and No!

First of all, let's consider what it means to be wealthy. You have a picture pop into your head when you hear the word "wealthy" and it will probably match up pretty well with dictionary definitions like, "very affluent"; "characterized by abundance"; or "having a great deal of money, resources or assets." But I'm not sure how practical or helpful those definitions are. Wealthy can mean different things to different people depending on a number of factors. Then again, just saying "wealth is relative" is not helpful either, especially if you want to set a goal and work toward being wealthy. So, let's consider some more practical definitions of wealth and see how Grandpa stacks up.

If you want to **make wealthy a number** the researchers who wrote *The Millionaire Next Door* have a formula. They suggest that you take your age, times it by your annual pre-tax (gross) income, then divide that by 10; that will give you your **expected net worth**. They then suggest that if your **actual net worth** (the value of your assets minus your debts) is in the top 25% of your expected net worth you are a prodigious accumulator of wealth (PAW). And if your actual net worth is twice your

> If you are 25 years old making $40,000 a year before taxes, your **expected net worth** is $100,000 (25 X $40,000 / 10). If your **actual net worth** is over $75,000 you are a PAW and if it is $200,000 you are wealthy (for a 25-year-old making $40,000).
>
> If you are 16 years old making $4000 a year before taxes, your **expected net worth** is $6400, you're a PAW if you have $4800 **in the bank** and wealthy if you have $12,800 (for a 16-year-old making $4000).
>
> If you're 60 years old making $76,000. Your **expected net worth** is $456,000 and you're a PAW at $342,000 and wealthy at $912,000 (for a 60-year-old making $76,000).

expected net worth, you are wealthy. As you can see from the examples in the text box, even with this formula, wealth is still relative depending on your age and income, but this allows you to measure wealth as a number.

If you want to **measure wealth by security**, you may want to turn to Richard Kiyosaki, the author of *Rich Dad, Poor Dad*. He defines wealth with a question, "If you stopped working today, how long could you survive financially at your current standard of living?" This definition suggests that your lifestyle (and your satisfaction with it) is a major factor in determining wealth. It's simple math. If your lifestyle costs $36,000 a year and you have $360,000 in the bank you could survive for 10 years.

> Your Great-grandma and Great-grandpa Hatch pose an interesting case study here. When they retired, they lived solely on their social security benefits, so they made a conscious decision to make their lifestyle simple and nomadic. **And more importantly they made it fun.** You should ask Grandma about that.

But that's not the whole story. Is your $360,000 earning money for you? If so, you could survive longer. And what about inflation? Every year prices go up. So, as your costs go up, your money gets used up faster (or else your lifestyle needs to change). And what if your $360,000 is not in the bank, but tied up in your home equity or in investments that tank? This definition, then, is not perfect, but I still think this is one of the most practical ways to measure wealth.

If you want to **define wealth by power**, Dave Ramsey of *The Total Money Makeover* fame has a great definition for you. He has written, "True wealth is about three things: making an impact through giving, leaving a legacy and having options for how you live your life." (*What is Wealth?*, Ramsey Solutions). If you accept the **definition of power** as "the ability to influence others or the course of events" (Oxford Dictionary), Ramsey makes good sense. Having a lot of money can allow you do to all of that!

But one of the reasons I love Dave Ramsey is that he doesn't just teach about how to handle money and gain wealth, he teaches you WHY you should do it. And he does it from a Biblical point of view. One of the things he teaches is that having lots of money doesn't make you good or bad, it just amplifies what you already are. If you are a generous, happy person, more money will help you be more generous and happier. If you are a greedy, unhappy person, more money will tempt you to be greedier and more miserable.

So, by Ramsey's definition of true wealth, when will you have enough money to be wealthy? When you have enough to help others become self-reliant, when you can leave your family better off than you were, and when you have options in your life. I hear echoes from the beginning of this book where I wrote about the principles of provident living and self-reliance. It doesn't take money, so much, as it takes the application of those principles and the grace and mercy of a loving God.

So, how does Grandpa stack up?

If you go by the **numbers**, I am a PAW, but not necessarily wealthy.

Judging by **security,** Grandma and I are very secure, with enough money coming in that we never have to work again. We also have contingency plans in place to deal with inflation and emergencies.

In terms of **power**, I consider myself to be very wealthy! I've made a powerful, positive impact all my life through the laws of tithing and the fast; and have given my money, time, effort and love through Church service, the Boy Scouts and other of my favorite causes. I've been able to help my family in times of stress and need – observing, of course, the principles of self-reliance and helping them maintain their dignity. Leaving a legacy **is** about financial things, but it can be much more. I have strived to teach my children correct spiritual and financial principles and let them govern themselves. That has served them better than any money or business they could have inherited from me and, in many cases, they have done better than I. And now, I am trying to do an even better job with you. When I consider the options available to me because I am self-reliant and blessed, I am afraid my problem is I have too many options. I sometimes can't decide which option is best.

So, while money isn't everything, it is something. And there is no question that the more wealth a good person accumulates, the better amplified their God-given gifts, talents, and options for service can be. I want you to have greater influence; leave an even better legacy; and be bothered with even more options than I. So, to that end, I offer to you my suggestions on how to become wealthy. Grandpa has a very simple recipe for becoming wealthy! It's simple, but certainly isn't easy or a lot more people would be wealthy. Just don't lose sight of the fact that ***it's not complicated***.

Grandpa's Recipe for Wealth
What you will need:
A measure of capital (the more the better)
An investment vehicle with a healthy RoR
Time
Patience
Directions:
1. Place capital in an investment vehicle with a healthy RoR.
2. Let earnings accumulate.
3. Fold earnings back into investment vehicle.
4. Add additional accumulated capital into investment vehicle.
5. Repeat steps 2-4 over and over and over until you are wealthy.
6. Be aware this will take time.

1. Adopt the proper attitudes about investing

Attitudes are the way we feel and act toward something without having to think about it. They cannot be created, but they can be formed, shaped and changed. I have a bad attitude toward any dairy product that has started to rot – like cottage cheese or yogurt. I don't know where the attitude came from and I don't care. Grandma really loves rotting dairy and thinks I am missing out. In like manner, we all have attitudes toward investing and they usually come from experiences that have shaped them.

When I was a kid, my parents told me that investing in the stock market was like gambling – just a way to lose all your money. I grew up with a fascination for the stock market, but had an attitude of distrust about it. In my twenties, I gave a stock broker $1000 to invest for me. He called me on the first day I was in the market and told me I had made $300 – a 30% return in just one day. I was thrilled. The next day he called me and told me I had lost $200. I freaked out, called him a crook, told him to cash out my account and send me my money. Although I was up 10% after just two days in the market, my negative attitude was reinforced.

Ten years later, a trusted friend advised me that I could make much more money in my retirement savings if I invested it in the stock market option rather than the interest-bearing option. I took his advice and shifted part of my account into a managed stock portfolio and forced myself to ignore it. When my quarterly statement came, I was blown away by the growth and moved almost all my money into that account. Listening to a trusted friend and having a positive experience changed my attitude.

When it comes to investing there are some attitudes you may need to shape and change. Here are a few of my favorite good attitudes about investing.

Saving money is good, but investing is better – way better. The goal is to get your money to wake up and go to work for you. Invest enough money in the right assets and you can quit worrying about working for money.

Invested earnings can be lost – and that is okay. Risk is a fact of investing life and you need to learn to deal with it. The higher your tolerance for risk, the higher your potential for earnings. It's also important to know the difference between losing part of your earnings and losing part of your principal (original investment). It's expected that from time you time you will lose part of your earnings, as long as you don't lose them all and start losing your principal.

There is a huge difference between taking an acceptable risk and paying the stupid tax. Although risk is part of the game, smart investors do what they can to minimize risk. Here are some suggestions learned from my alma matter, the School of Hard Knocks.

- Before you invest, do your research, then do some more research, then do even more research. Know, for sure, what you are getting into.
- When you start an investment, it's best to "dip your toe" in the water rather than jump in over your head.
- If an investment sounds too good to be true (or even close to it), it probably is. Take a pass.
- Have at least one person on your "team" who is a little bit pessimistic and/or cynical and give them a healthy amount of credence.

Time is a crucial when it comes to investing – make it your friend rather than your foe. Compounded interest grows exponentially over time. Real estate investing is the long game. Portfolio losses recover with time. Start investing early and give yourself enough time to be successful.

Withdrawing money from your investment account is stupid – don't do it. The success cycle is invest, earn, compound; invest, earn, compound; invest… (you get the idea). Break this cycle and you will be sorry.

2. Accumulate capital

Earlier in this book, I defined capital as "anything you own that gives you economic value, opportunity or advantage." It is the stuff that you can put to work to create wealth. It's the stuff dreams are made of. The more capital you invest the better your chances of accumulating wealth so, **get capital and get a lot of it!**

There are many kinds of capital, but the basic form is money. Money is a medium of exchange that everyone understands and accepts. It is easy to use.

Your greatest source of **capital is your paycheck.** Do not misunderstand me, I am not saying having a big income will make you rich. There are many people that made lots of money, but never really became wealthy and many people who made modest incomes who did. But having a big income can make accumulating capital easier.

So, get (or create) a good job, do a good job and get paid well. This idea of getting paid well is well illustrated by an example from my life. When I worked for the Church Educational System (CES), I was paid well, but my CES salary was not all that went into being paid well. With CES my work and education were acknowledged and rewarded; my family was provided with affordable, top-notch medical and financial benefits and we were given training and advice on how to manage them; and there was a well-thought-out and well-funded compensation plan with job security. If I wanted to work in the summer to make extra money, CES provided me with opportunities. CES cared about my family and included

Grandma in trainings, symposiums, tours, workshops and an annual getaway. And CES kept every promise they ever made to me. Whatever you choose to do for a living, make sure you are "paid well." Yes, I'm talking about money, but I am also talking about all the other things that make a job "good". And when you **are** blessed to be "paid well" appreciate it and be very careful about losing it.

Okay now, back to capital! Get (or create) a good job, do a good job and get paid well!

Any time you get paid you can start accumulating capital by paying yourself second. Remember**, at least** 10% of your gross income needs to go into building wealth through investment. If you are serious about producing wealth you will want to contribute a greater percentage of your income, you will also want to add money from windfalls (like birthday cash, tax returns etc.) and perhaps work a part-time job or side hustle.

Now a word about obsession – is it good or bad? Your ability to accumulate capital is tied directly to your intensity. When talking about getting out of debt, Dave Ramsey talks about "gazelle intensity." The book of Proverbs suggests that if you want to get free from a bad agreement you've made (like debt), you need to act like a gazelle that's running from a hunter. (Great picture, huh!) I agree with Dave that you should be Gazelle intense when getting out of debt, but once you are out of debt should you apply this same intensity to accumulating capital?

> My son, if you have put up security for your neighbor, if you have shaken hands in pledge for a stranger, you have been trapped by what you said, ensnared by the words of your mouth.
>
> So do this, my son, to free yourself, since you have fallen into your neighbor's hands: **Go—to the point of exhaustion—** and give your neighbor no rest!
>
> Allow no sleep to your eyes, no slumber to your eyelids. Free yourself, **like a gazelle from the hand of the hunter,** like a bird from the snare of the fowler.
> Proverbs 6: 1-5 (Emphasis added)

There are people today called F.I.R.E. Followers. F.I.R.E. is an acronym for Financial Independence Retire Early. These people are gazelle intense, with some contributing 75% of their income into savings and investments. At that rate they accumulate lots of capital fast and they plan to retire at a very young age. Needless to say, they are living very, very frugally.

Remember Grandpa's story about living alone in Salt Lake while Grandma was recuperating from surgery at her parents' place in Idaho? I lived like a hermit for six weeks and loved it, but as soon as Grandma came home, we went back to our normal, balanced life. I suggest you live a little bit south of normal. **Don't** live so frugally that you miss out on the joy of life or fail to take care of your family but **do** live so frugally that you are considered different. Be serious and diligent about saving and investing.

> BTW, with a reasonable return, you could turn that $2700 a year into over $500,000 over 30 years.

You can accumulate capital even on a modest salary. Let's suppose you work at a fast-food joint making $13 an hour. How much capital could you accumulate? At $13 an hour you'll make about $2250 a month or $27,000 a year. If you find a way to live on that salary and save 10% for wealth building, you'd accumulate $2700 a year. (That's not bad considering that a recent report said most American households don't even have $500 in savings for emergencies.) It would be really difficult to live on $27,000 a year and I am not suggesting you try it, but as you can see it's possible to accumulate capital on a modest salary if you are disciplined enough.

But guess what? You are not going to flip burgers the rest of your life. You're going to get a good education and experience so you can get (or create) a good job; you're going to work hard so you get promotions and raises or grow your business; and you're going to be paid well, because you'll proactively manage your career. And your ability to amass capital will be amazing.

3. Invest your capital

Repeat after me, "saving is good, but investing is better." Money stuffed under a mattress or buried in a coffee can in the backyard is kind of good, but it could be stolen, forgotten or decompose. Cash saved in a checking or savings account is better, but it is asleep at best and could be used to buy dangerous devil's tools. The best place for saved money is in investment vehicles, where it is awake and working for you.

There is a very wide range of ways to invest your money and whole books written on each type of investment and how to use them. If you are interested you can study hard and become an expert, but my explanations and advice to you will be simple – enough to get you started.

Let's start with some basic investment principals

Don't interrupt the investment cycle. The investment cycle is: invest, earn, compound; invest, earn, compound; etc., etc., etc. This is the cycle that allows you to take advantage of the power of compounding. Remember the story of the farrier and the rich rancher where one penny turned into over $83,000 in a couple of hours? The farrier was wise enough to let that penny compound over and over and over. Now, he was making 100% interest per nail, which is pure fantasy, but the principle is the same. Let me ask you this. What if after the eighth nail, the farrier had taken a dollar out of his earnings and bought a pop from the vending machine in the barn? How much would that have affected his earnings? You guess while I tell you a real-life story.

I have a retirement investment account that I started in 1982 and have never converted to income – it's still earning money. Several times over the years, I have ignorantly broken the "interrupting the cycle" rule and dipped into that account. The first was in 1986 when I withdrew $5000 to buy a van for our family. The second was in 1990 when I took $7000 out to pay for termite damage on our home so we could sell it. The third time was in 2003 when I used $10,000 to buy a vending machine business. That is a total of $23,000. I just ran the numbers and discovered that if I had left that money in the retirement account, I would have an additional $239,000 in that account today. Withdrawing $23,000 cost me $239,000.

Now that is a sad story, but sadder still is that, because I didn't understand this rule until much later than 2003, I dipped into that account other times and for much more money than $23,000. **Even sadder still** is that my figures do not take into account the money I had to pay in taxes and penalties for withdrawing money from a tax deferred account. (More on that later.) **Even sadder still** is that not one of those withdrawals was even close to an emergency, just dumb tax after dumb tax. Don't be impulsive. Don't be sad. Invest your money and let the cycle do its job.

By the way, that $1 bottle of Mountain Dew would have cost the farrier over $65,000.

Interest and Time can be your biggest friends or worst enemies. The famous physicist Albert Einstein is credited with saying, "Compound interest is the eighth wonder of the world. He who understands it, earns it … he who doesn't … pays it." I've already beat this subject to death, but it needs to be deader. **Paying** compound interest is bad. **Earning** compound interest is good. Understand this! Apply this! Roll all of your investment earnings back into investment and make money on your money, on your money.

Grandpa's corollary to Dr. Einstein's compound interest statement is, "Time is the most powerful force in finance. He who uses it, wins; he who doesn't, loses." When it comes to wealth building, time is your friend and the younger you are, the better of a friend it is, because the longer your money is in the investment cycle the greater your chances of accumulating wealth. Start investing NOW!

And if you want to see real power – *synergize.* If you take the power of compound interest and the power of time and use them together you have just gone nuclear! *(Very funny grandpa! Einstein going nuclear!)*

> **BIG WORD WARNNG**
> Synergistic effect is when two things work together to produce a greater effect than if they worked separately.

Watch your RoR. Simply stated, the higher your RoR, the greater your chances of accumulating wealth. Rate of

> **RoR Math**
> Sold Stock for $150
> Bought Stock for $100
> Profit $ 50
> $50 / $100 = **50% RoR**

Return (RoR) is the net gain or loss taken on an investment, stated as a percentage of the initial cost. For example, if I buy a stock for $100 and sell it for $150, my profit is $50. And since $50 is 50% of $100 (initial cost), my RoR is 50%.

Is 50% a good RoR? Well, that depends on other factors like how long I held the stock before I sold; were there any other gains (like dividends) or costs (fees, commissions, interest) involved in buying, holding or selling the stock. Keep it simple by asking yourself two questions.

The first question is: **What can I reasonably expect to earn on this investment?** The key word here is **"reasonably."** Some returns are easy to anticipate – like a certificate of deposit (CD). Other investments will require some research. I'm not asking you to become a professional investment analysist, but I am asking you to do your **"due diligence."** This means you do everything you can to understand an investment. Is it safe? Is it affordably priced? What has it earned in the past and can I expect similar returns in the future?

The second question is: **What is this investment going to cost me?** Every investment comes at a cost in addition to your initial investment. Stocks may have commissions; mutual funds have loads; managed accounts have fees, businesses take your time; and **every** investment, even money put into simple savings accounts, has opportunity costs. What I am asking you to do is count those costs and make sure the investment is affordable for you and worth the cost. (I have put together a brief glossary of some of the most common cost in the text box below.)

Expense Ratio – Annual cost of owning some investments. It pays for management fees, administrative fees and other costs. It is calculated as a percentage of your balance and is deducted from your account as long as you own the investment.

Commission – Charged by brokers or sales people as their pay for helping you buy and sell investments. A commission can be charged each time you buy or sell an investment. Sometimes the fee is a percentage of the transaction and sometimes it is a flat fee.

Load – Sales charge or commission paid when buying or selling mutual fund shares. This compensates brokers or financial advisors for selling you the fund. Loads can be front-end (charged when buying), back-end (charged when selling), level (charged annually).

Redemption Fee – Charged to investors who only hold their mutual share funds for a short period of time before selling. It discourages frequent trading and protects long-term traders. The fees usually go back into the fund, not to brokers, advisors or fund company.

Penalty – Monetary sanctions imposed for breaking a rule or a law. There are many examples, but the most common one for you would be withdrawing money from a certificate of deposit before it matures.

Management Fee – Levied by an investment manager for overseeing certain investment funds. It compensates them for the time, experience, judgement and expenses as they try to make more money for you.

Acquisition Fee – Payment to fund managers, investment companies, lenders or lessors for identifying, researching and acquiring property, funding or investments and protecting you in the process.

Opportunity Costs -- An opportunity cost is the **value of what you could have had instead** when you make a decision. If you choose to invest in XYZ you have to ask yourself what you're giving up to make that investment.

There are three reasons for going to all this trouble. One is to **keep you from paying the stupid tax** (getting ripped off); two is to **help you get more bang out of your investment** and three is to keep your **expectations realistic.** Let me show you what I mean with an example.

Let's say you've decided to invest $100 each month and your options for investment are an interest-bearing growth CD (paying 5%) or a mutual fund (which has averaged 8% over the last 20 years). Let's see how much you'd accumulate over 20 years (supposing the mutual fund hit the 8% target and CD interest rate remains the same).

- The 5% CD will accumulate $41,105.27
- The 8% mutual fund will accumulate $58,931.33

Over twenty years, the mutual fund accumulates almost $18,000 more.

But wait, to keep our expectations realistic we need to take into account that the mutual fund has fees and the CD doesn't. And in this case, you've selected a mutual fund that deducts a 1% level-load from your account balance each year. What does that fee do to our bottom line after 20 years?

- The 5% CD will still accumulate $41,105.27
- The 8% mutual fund will accumulate $51,615.19

That fee reduces your mutual fund earnings by over $7300, but it still outperforms the CD by over $10,000.

There are many more factors we could consider in this example, but this should give you a feeling for how doing your research and thinking an investment through can help you make better and more confident investment decisions. In this case, the mutual fund **reasonably and realistically** seems to afford you the best RoR.

Understand your risk tolerance and deal with it. In general, risk tolerance is how comfortable you are with doing something – like rappelling off the side of a mountain or going on a blind date. While it is often helpful to be brave and try new things, high risk is not necessary to be good or successful. It is also important to understand that some things you feel uncomfortable with (like Halloween haunted houses) have minor consequences, while others (like skydiving) could have major consequences.

Investing your money is one of those areas of major consequence. You can earn a lot of money, but you can lose a lot too. Some people are paralyzed by fear when it comes to investing while others get a buzz, but most of us are somewhere in the middle. We want to do it, make some good returns, but not lose our money.

Risk is a fact of life when it comes to investing. The more risk you're willing to take, the greater the **potential** returns and losses. Suppose a car rental company wants to borrow money to help rescue their business that has not been doing well; or XYZ Energy's geologists believe they've found a new oil deposit in North Dakota, and they want investors to fund their drilling; or an American company wants to start making semiconductors to compete with the huge Chinese firms and they need startup money. All of these are examples of high-risk investments because if the ventures fail, investors could lose part or all of their money, but the companies are willing to pay investors a lot **IF** they are successful. On the other hand, if I put my money in a savings account at my credit union, it is very safe (insured by the government, even), but the credit union will pay me less than 1% interest because they have all kinds of people who will put their money in a savings account and they can pull it out whenever they want.

As an investor you will take some opportunities and pass on others, depending on how you tolerate risk in general and view specific investments. If your risk tolerance is low, you can still invest, but you will need to follow some important strategies. If you have a high tolerance for risk, you may need to put some guidelines in place to protect yourself. While there is no right answer for everyone, there will always be a right answer for you.

It will take some time and experience as an investor before you can really know your risk tolerance, but at least you can go into investing with your "eyes wide open." Give careful and consistent thought to the following questions.

- What is my overall financial position and how much can I afford to lose at this time? The better your financial situation, the more risk you can assume.

- What are my investing goals and where am I in my progress? If you are looking to have $2 million to retire on, you will be more likely to take risks when you're 25 (and have lots of time to recover from a loss), than when you are 60.

- What are my expectations and are they realistic? A return of 5% can be earned easily and safely, but it will take you over 14 years to double your investment. On the other hand, being offered a 25% annual return is exciting, but the risk of loss is much higher.

One other very important thing you need to get a handle on before you really know your risk tolerance is how you **actually react** to gains and losses – especially losses. I've already told the story about my first foray into stock investing – losing $200 freaked me out and kept me out of the market for 10 years. Since that time, I have come a long way in dealing with investment loss, but it still gets to me. A couple of years ago I tried day trading. I failed because I couldn't

> **Day trading is a form of investing in which individuals buy and sell investments on the same day. The goal is to make money with short-term trades. It's fast paced and requires strategy and decision-making skills.**

keep my emotions in check. If I had a big loss I would freak out, start making stupid trades and lose a lot of money. Unfortunately, you will not be able to gauge your emotional reaction to investment losses until you've had a few.

No matter your tolerance for risk, you can still be a successful investor. The key is to have a strategy (or several) to deal with risk. Here are some suggestions.

- **Diversify** your investments. This means you spread your capital out over **different asset classes** (bonds, stocks, commodities, real estate, etc.); **different industries** (energy, materials, technology, healthcare, etc.) and **different parts of the world**. If one class, industry or region does poorly, most likely others will do better and your chance of a big loss is minimized.

> **The 100-minus-your-age Rule** says subtracting your age from 100 gives you the percentage of your portfolio that should be in moderate or high-risk investments. A 25-year-old could have 75% in higher risk investments, but a 70-year-old should have only 30%.

- **Balance** your investments. Have some of your money in low-risk investments, moderate-risk investments and high-risk investments. (More about this later.) That way you can have the benefit of both safety and earnings. How much you decide to put in each risk category depends on your investment goals, your risk tolerance and where you are on your investment journey. Consider the 100-minus-your-age Rule.

- **De-emotionalize** your investing. I've already talked about the emotions that can come with investment loss – anger, resentment, embarrassment, demonic posession. But there is another side to emotional investing and that is when you are making big gains and feeling greedy or fear missing out. If your investment has given you great returns, greed and fear of missing out may influence you to stay in an investment too long. The best ways to de-emotionalize investing are to have set of **fast, hard rules** that you follow and to have an **investment partner** that helps keep you level headed about opportunities, gains and losses.

- **Adjust** your investments. At least yearly, you will want to analyze how well each of your investments is doing and reallocate your money as needed to keep your investments balanced and maximize your returns.

- **Plan** your investments. This really should have been the first bullet point, but I thought if I started talking about planning again your brain might shut off. The worst time to make changes in your investment strategy is when things are going

> Be careful when you choose an investment advisor – they are not all created equal. People just starting out in the business may have a good heart and your best interests in mind, but they may not have the knowledge and experience of a seasoned professional. All investment advisors get paid, but be aware that some get paid, by companies they represent, for "selling" you certain product and services, while others are paid, by you, according to how well your investments do. Who do you think will be most worried about how well your investments do?

poorly, so have a well-thought-out plan, with loss contingencies in place, **before** you start investing. This is where a mentor or someone with some experience and education in investing (like a seasoned investment advisor) can be very helpful to you.

Remember, if you ever find yourself in doubt or feel stressed, it's okay to retreat into safer territory and live to invest another day. And remember you are always going to do your research and be a little cynical about any new investments. You'll worry less if you do your due diligence. Know what you are getting into and what a realistic RoR will be. Invest wisely and then stay the course.

Get on with your life. In our farrier's story, when he was getting a nail-by-nail report on how his pay was coming, he became distracted and stressed. So, what did he do? He asked the rancher to just keep the tally quietly so he could concentrate on the job. When he was finished, he was overwhelmed by how much he'd earned. Do the same thing!

One of the best pieces of advice I can give you about investing is to get on with your life. Get a life. Take care of your life. Enjoy it. And let the investments take care of themselves.

This will require you to both remember and forget at the same time. Remember that you have investments and check on them regularly. Forget that you have investments and let them do the work. Think of your money as an employee. Set "him" up for success and then let him do his job. You'll want to check in on him at regular intervals, but don't micromanage him. As your investments grow, you may want to hire a smart, experienced manager and let them manage your money – pay them to handle the stress.

Now we are ready to talk about the logistics of investing.

Have a plan. This first step should not come to you as a surprise. Start with a simple plan that will grow with your experience and capital and may change from year to year. To make it easy – just answer these questions.

- How much and how often will you be investing?
- What is your purpose and what are your SMART investment goals?
- What is your level of risk tolerance and what are your risk tolerance strategies?
- In which investment(s) will you be investing?
- What are your realistic expectations when it comes to RoR?
- How, and when, will you be assessing your progress and making adjustments?

Get organized. Before you invest you need to get your "ducks in a row." You not only need to be organized, but have an organization – individuals and institutions to help. Going it alone is not only inadvisable but, in some ways, impossible. Surround yourselves with a team that shares your vision. Your support team will start small and grow with your investments.

Start with your **parents.** Share your goals with them and ask for their help. They may feel somewhat inadequate and if they do, have them read this book (or others I have referenced) with you.

In addition, you may want to find an **investment buddy**. This would be someone on a similar investing path that you can talk things though with and who can hold you accountable.

Once you have some experience and knowledge, you may want to find **a mentor**. A mentor is a more experienced someone who teaches, advises and helps you along your investment path. It will take some effort to search out and secure help from the right person. It needs to be someone who knows what they are doing, who will get close to you, understand your goals and wants you to succeed.

I have an additional word or two of caution about mentors!

> **Emotional carpet bagger is Grandpa's term for people who prey on your emotions for their personal gain. Chief among them are people promoting multi-level-marketing schemes (MLMs). And there are some of these in the financial services industry. Be careful!**

First of all, there is a difference between a mentor and an emotional carpet bagger. There are many people out there who would love to "mentor" you but whose real goal is to make money off of you or use you. Be careful and prayerful in your choice of a mentor.

Second of all, being a mentee requires humility and gratitude. Although I have associated with good people and have received a lot of help in my life – for which I am grateful, I've never had a mentor. I was never humble enough to have a mentor. I had a hard time ever admitting I wasn't the smartest person in the room, admitting that I needed help, or taking other peoples' advice. If you really want the help of a mentor – choose carefully, ask sincerely and follow humbly.

In addition to a mentor, you will eventually need the assistance of others and many of them will be professionals. You may want a banker, a broker, a real estate agent, an insurance agent, an investment analysist, a tax advisor, an attorney, a fund manager and others. But as you begin you will get most of your professional help through two financial institutions – your bank or credit union and your investment brokerage.

You will need a financial institution for your money to rest and pass through on its way to work. This is a good time to talk about the difference between banks and credit unions. Some people claim that banks offer more options and greater safety, but neither of those things is true. Good credit unions offer as many options as banks and have the same level of deposit insurance ($250,000). The **big difference** is in the reasons banks and credit unions exist. Banks exist to make a profit for their owners, while credit unions are not-for-profit organizations owned by their depositors. As you can imagine, that single difference is huge when it comes to the practices and policies of the two, especially when it comes to serving their customers, with credit unions winning. Grandpa has used both banks and credit unions and prefers credit unions hands down, but you will need to choose for yourself. Shop for the institution that has the best services, fee structure and meets your needs. Your bank or credit union needs to have some basic elements. It needs to afford you checking privileges, multiple sub-accounts and savings options.

You may choose to have some investment accounts at your bank or credit union, but most of your investment accounts with be with an investment brokerage that will help you invest in other instruments. When Grandpa was young, investors used a broker to buy and sell investments. We had very little oversight. We basically chose a broker and trusted him. Today, with deregulation and the invention of the Internet, investors can basically DIY. You still go through a brokerage (they have the licenses and exchange memberships needed to buy investments) but you have the option of "hiring" a full-service broker **or** using a discount brokerage where you can research, buy, track and sell investments on your own. If you start your investment journey using a tax-advantaged investment plan (explained below) your broker will be selected for you. Otherwise, you will have to open your own account with the brokerage of your choice.

If you are younger than 18 years old, you will need to have your parents establish these accounts for you. They will be yours, but will be considered custodial accounts. This is the law, but even if it weren't, I would have suggested it. You can benefit from your parents help and guidance.

You can research brokers and brokerages online, but you will want all the help you can get in the process. Talk with family, friends and mentors that have experience with investment accounts. Have your parents or mentors help you in your search. The University of Google is a great place to learn about this process, but learn about it with the help of parents or mentors. Once you have decided which firm to use, setting up and funding are simple.

Use a tax-advantaged investment plan. One of the financial goals you will **all** have is to have a nice, big cash account to live on when you quit working for money (i.e. a retirement fund). So, one of the earliest investment vehicles to start with is a retirement savings plan that you can contribute to your whole working career.

Retirement savings plans are not investments in themselves; they are vehicles that help you invest. Tax law allows you to have retirement saving plans with special, tax-friendly advantages. You can set one up yourself or your employer can offer it as a benefit. They're a wonderful way to start investing – simple to use, with many advantages. Here is a quick summary of the two most popular:

- **401Ks** are retirement plans set up by employers. The employer contracts with a broker to offer employees a menu of investment and management options. Employees' contributions come right out of their paychecks and some employers encourage investing by **matching** part of employees' contributions. Best of all, employees are not taxed on investment earnings until they withdraw them, letting them compound and earn more money. Another upside to 401Ks is that they are portable. If you change jobs, you can take all of your contributions and earnings, and part or all of your employer's contributions, with you.

- **Individual Retirement Accounts (IRAs)** are investment plans **you set up for yourself** through a bank, credit union or broker (usually because your employer doesn't offer a 401K). They are very similar to 401Ks with a variety of investments, automatic contribution options and the same tax advantages. There are a couple of downsides when it comes to IRAs. 1) There is no employer match. 2) You can only contribute to an IRA a third of what you can to a 401K.

It is hard to imagine a better set up than these tax-advantaged investment plans. They help make investment appealing, convenient and automatic; you keep all your earnings in the investment account for better compounding; and, in the case of 401Ks, you can get free money from your boss. One of the few downsides is that eventually the government is going to want you to pay taxes on your money. But what if you could get out of paying taxes on your earnings? The good news is, you can – if you use a Roth retirement plan.

401Ks and IRAs each come in two flavors – traditional and Roth. Under **traditional plans** you don't pay taxes on your contributions or your earnings **until you withdraw them from the plan**. Under a **Roth plan** your **contributions are taxed before they go into the plan**, but your **earnings are not taxed when you pull them out.**

Grandpa highly recommends the Roth flavor!

You don't need to use a tax-advantaged investment plan, but not having to pull money out of the investment cycle to pay taxes is HUGE! And if you're smart, you can leverage Roth plans even more effectively. For example, if you're contributing to a Roth plan while your children are still dependents, you'll be benefiting from deductions and credits that can greatly reduce your tax liability, making taxes on contributions virtually nothing. Hence, little or no tax on your contributions and no tax on your investment earnings.

I have one word of warning about tax-advantaged plans. They are not piggy banks. The government designed them as long-term, consistent, retirement savings plans and consequently, if you withdraw your money from either plan before you turn 59 ½, you'll have to pay the full tax **and** a penalty. There are some exceptions to this rule, but generally it is best to not withdraw your money.

Pick your investments. When you go to a nice museum you can bet that what's on display is not everything the museum owns. There are many more artifacts in storage, on tour, or lent out to other museums. The person who manages and cares for all of that stuff, designs the exhibits, and displays the artifacts is called a curator.

The investment world is a lot like a museum. Some investment vehicles, like stocks, are on constant display and get a lot of attention. Others, like real estate, sit quietly in corners. Others are hidden away and the majority of people never see them. The variety of ways to invest your money is mind blowing and there is no way we can discuss all the options in this book, so Grandpa is going to serve as your investment museum curator. The name of the exhibit I have curated for you is called:

The Beginners Guide to Investing

Investing doesn't need to be complicated or difficult. As a matter of fact, there are many, many people that have gained wealth using **only** simple and easy investments. In this guide we will talk about easy, basic investments that will get you started. It will be up to you to study and learn about other options and chart your own path in adulthood.

When you are very young, your first "investing" duty will be to amass capital. You will need a place to collect it and put it to work from the beginning. And even when you are older, you may need a place to park your money between investments. A good place to do these things is a certificate of deposit.

Certificate of Deposit (CD)

- ***What is it?*** You can buy a certificate at a bank or credit union and hold it for a set term (usually 3 months to 6 years) with a set interest rate.

- ***What is the RoR?*** CD interest rates move with the price of money, usually paying about the same as the Federal Reserve charges banks to borrow money. I've seen CD rates over 11% and as low as .9%, but your rate doesn't change during the term of the CD.

- ***What does it cost?*** There are no commissions or fees, but there is the opportunity cost of tying up your money for the term of the certificate because if you pull your money out before it matures, you will have to pay a penalty.

- ***Why is this a good investment?*** You don't get any safer than this – you only lose money if you pull it out too soon. It's an excellent investment for saving buckets you are not planning on spending or investing right way. It's convenient and easy to use. It compounds your interest monthly to give you slightly better growth. Sometimes, CDs offer very competitive returns – especially when the Federal Reserve interest rates are high or banks or credit unions offer a bonus to attract deposits.

When you are ready, the best place to start investing is in the financial markets. I believe that the U.S. financial markets have created more wealth and wealthy people than any other types of investments. Financial markets are marketplaces where investors buy and sell **stocks** (ownership shares in a company), **bonds** (loans to a company or governments), **money** (currency and money funds), or **commodities** (raw materials like gold or wheat). It's all done electronically and can be done through any brokerage. Grandpa suggests you pick your first investments from the following list.

Money Market Fund (MMF)

- ***What is it?*** Not to be confused with a money market account at banks, a Money Market Fund (MMF) is actually a mutual fund (see below) that invests in really low-risk, money-based investments. MMF shares are usually bought and sold at $1 and as your shares earn interest it is either credited to your account or used to buy you more $1 shares.

- ***What is the RoR?*** MMF interest rates are pretty comparable to CD rates. They may change daily, depending on economic conditions, but they are usually pretty stable.

- ***What does it cost?*** You buy MMFs through a broker and they usually charge expense ratio fees ranging from .07 to .16% of your account balance that are deducted periodically during the year.

- ***Why is this a good investment?*** These are just a little riskier than CDs, but there is a very small chance that you can lose principle. MMFs are highly liquid with no penalties for early withdrawal and interest is compounded daily, maximizing compounding. Like CDs, MMFs are an excellent investment for saving buckets or money you are waiting to invest in something else.

Pooled Investment Vehicles

Pooled investment vehicles are a way to share the expenses; simplify the choices and reduce the risks of investing by pooling your money with other investors. Instead of buying a single share of Microsoft stock, you can take that $500 and buy two shares of the Fidelity 500 Index Fund (FXAIX) which invests in Microsoft, Apple, NVIDIA, Amazon, Meta, Alphabet, Berkshire Hathway and Tesla – just to name a few. This fund is managed according to a well-researched strategy; there is built-in diversification; and when you're ready, you can just sell your shares in the fund. Grandpa suggests that, early on in your investment career, you start investing with some type of pooled investment vehicle. You can buy these through your tax-advantaged investment plan or directly through a broker. Just be sure you research the plan investments, costs and past performance before you buy. Here are a few examples of pooled investment vehicles.

Mutual Fund (MF)

- *What is it?* Mutual Funds (MFs) are portfolios of stocks, bonds and other securities managed by professional money managers. Our FXAIX example above is a mutual fund. There is usually a minimum investment of $500 to $5000 required, depending on the fund.

- *What is the RoR?* The return on MFs can be significantly higher than CDs or Money Market Funds, without a significant increase in risk. Over the last 15 years, the average return on mutual funds invested in the stock market have averaged between 8 and 10%. **(Caution: Past performance does not guarantee future results.)**

- *What does it cost?* MFs generally charge three types of fees. An **expense ratio** is an annual fee (.5 to 1.5%) that covers the administrative cost of the fund. **A load** is the one-time commission (3 to 6%) paid to brokers and advisors. A **redemption fee** (1 to 2%) may be charged if you sell your shares within a short period of time. Competition has brought these fees down over the years and every fund will offer you a different fee structure, so shop them.

- *Why is this a good investment?* MFs allow you to invest in the market in a safe and profitable way – affording you diversity, professional management and reduced investment costs. If you shop the fees and hold onto your shares for the long term, MFs can work really well for you. But you do have to shop for the right fund.

Exchanged Traded Fund (ETF)

- *What is it?* Exchange-traded funds (ETFs) are investment funds made up of multiple assets. They are bought and sold on financial exchanges, like an individual stock (so the price can go up or down during the trading day). They have lower fees (because they are not so closely managed) and you can get into an EFT for just the cost of a single share. They also have a slightly better tax advantage.

- **What is the RoR?** EFTs have not been around as long as mutual funds and don't have the same track record, but it appears that they average returns comparable to mutual funds. **(Remember: Past performance does not guarantee future results.)** But EFTs have lower fees and tax advantages that leave more of your money in the investment cycle.

- **What does it cost?** EFTs do not charge a load or any type of commission. And because of the way they are bought, sold and managed, their **expense ratio** can be much lower (often less than .25%)

  - **Why is this a good investment?** EFTs allow you many of the advantages of MFs including safety, diversification and reduced investment costs. Shop for lower fees to keep more money in the invest cycle. Plan to hold onto your shares for the long term.

Real Estate Investment Trust (REIT)

- **What is it?** Real Estate Investment Trusts (REITs) are created when companies sell shares to raise real estate investment capital. This allows small investors the option of investing in real estate without putting out a lot of money

> Volatility is how often and how far asset prices go up and down. High volatility can be good if you are a day trader (because you can make money when assets go up or down), but long-haul investors like to see low volatility.

or having their money tied up for years. They also tend to be less volatile than other pooled assets. And REITs are required to pay 90% of their profits back to investors in dividends.

> Dividends are like getting a bonus. When companies make a profit, they sometimes pay part of that profit to investors in the form of *dividends.*

- **What is the RoR?** REITs tend to pay a little better than MFs or ETFs because they earn money from both dividends and appreciation.

- **What does it cost?** REIT expense ratios are similar to mutual funds, but other fees can be pricier – including management fees (as high as 5%) and acquisition fees (1 to 2%).

- **Why is this a good investment?** You pay slighter higher fees but the tradeoff is the stability of real estate as an investment and a better return.

HIGHER RISK
Cryptocurrency
Derivatives
Speculative Stocks & Funds
Junk Bonds

MODERATE RISK
Growth Stocks
Small Cap Stocks
Medium-rated Bonds
Aggressive Mutual Funds

LIMITED RISK
Real Estate
Blue Chip Stocks
High-Rate Bonds
Conservative Mutual Funds
Government Bonds and Notes

LOWER RISK
Savings Accounts
Money Market Funds
Treasury Bills
Annuities

Good News: Huge growth potential, excitement.
Bad News: Much higher risk, principal at risk.

Good News: Much better growth, use of potential.
Bad News: Higher risk and loss of liquidity.

Good News: Security, liquidity, better growth.
Bad News: Opportunity cost and wasted potential.

Good News: Safety and liquidity.
Bad News: Can actually lose ground to inflation.

As you can see in this chart, the investments I just suggested fall into the limited risk or moderate risk range (conservative or aggressive mutual funds). This is the time in your life when you can be a little more daring. You will most likely see some good growth, but if you incur a loss, you have plenty of time to recover.

Wade into investing. Your entry into investing should be much like a foray into a mountain lake. Take your time and become accustomed to the temperature of the water, but by all means, wade in. Just learning, thinking and planning about investing won't make you any money. Be smart, deliberate and careful, but by all means work your plan and invest.

If you are wise, you'll get a lot of help from your team. Have them walk through the logistics with you. Heck, you can even ask your grandpa for help. Just be sure they know what they are talking about and if you ever feel uncomfortable with their advice – walk away.

Stick with your investing plan. "Time in the market" is a strategy that has made more people rich than any other. This means you get in early and stay in for the long term. It's alright to change or move investments as part of a well-planned strategy, but pulling your money out because the market is going down or because you are trying to "time (outsmart) the market" just pulls your money out the investment cycle and is seldom beneficial.

Review, adjust and grow. You don't want to obsess over your investments, but you need to have a plan to review your progress regularly and make adjustments when necessary. For example, if your stocks are overperforming and it looks like the stock market might be headed for a correction, you might want to move some of your money over to a bond-based fund (because when stocks go down, bonds go up).

Grandpa! I though you said this was simple!?!

Don't worry so much about what I just said. Just remember that as you gain experience you will learn more about how the market works and how to do this. In the meantime, if you choose a managed fund, the manager will make these adjustments for you. It will cost a little more, but should pay off in bigger returns. But even then, you will review your quarterly statements and see how your investments are doing. Once you have some experience and are comfortable, you can learn about and branch out into other types of investments.

Now before we leave the subject of investing, I want to leave you with four very general thoughts.

Thought One: There is an old "tongue-in-cheek" adage that the way to make money investing is to buy low and sell high. This is supposed to be funny, because it's so obvious, but honestly there is a lot of wisdom in it. You will never know when an investment vehicle is at its lowest price, but often investments do go "on sale." Learn to be patient and wait for opportunities. Conversely, you will never know when an investment will peak, but almost all investments will eventually hit resistance and level out or lose value. Learn to take reasonable, healthy profit and get out – leaving something for others.

Thought Two: You've probably figured out that in the investment recipe the more capital you invest, the higher your ROR, and the longer you are in investments, the more likely you are to become wealthy. But I want you to remember the fable of *The Tortoise and the Hare* and work surely and consistently toward your investment goals. Increased capital will come with steady and consistent saving and compounding. Higher ROR will be more likely when you have gained experience and risk tolerance. Time in the market, however, will only come with time in the market. Start investing early and stay in it for the long run.

Thought Three: Remember that before you start to invest you should have an emergency fund established. When you are young, your emergency fund won't amount to much, but as you get out on your own and gain more responsibility, you'll need to make sure you have a fully funded (three to six month) emergency fund. If you have to stop investing for a while to build up or replenish your emergency fund, do it. Nothing will derail your investing efforts or tempt you to dip into your investment fund more than a serious emergency.

Thought Four: I left some popular investment items off the beginner's list on purpose, and I'd like to tell you why. I left precious metals (gold, silver, etc.) off the list because I don't see them as an investment. They seldom go on sale, so the only way you make money is to hold on to them for years. Precious metals do serve as a hedge against inflation, so you may want to buy some as a sort of emergency money storage. But don't plan on getting rich by buying them.

I also left life insurance off the list. The basic job of life insurance is to provide money to your loved ones if you pass away prematurely, but some insurance products have saving and investment elements built into them. Although some of those policies have been touted as a smart and safe way to invest and the idea has some merit, I think there are better ways for beginners to invest. I will talk more about this in our subsection on protecting what you have and love.

The other investment I left off the beginner's list was real estate. I love real estate as an investment and stealthy wealth builder – it goes on sale from time to time; it's a fantastic way to apply leverage; and hard to lose money on if you invest right. However, to be done right, real estate investments need to be held for

> **Leverage is the tactic of using other people's money to make money (like a mortgage). It is not a strategy I recommend for beginning investors, but when you know what you're doing, it can be a great financial ladder if used correctly.**

111

the long term. Buying, holding and selling real estate come with significant costs and you make money in real estate through rents and appreciation, which both take time to accumulate. So, if you only hold real estate for the short term, you incur the costs without the benefit of the earnings. If you want to invest in real estate as a beginner, look at REITs. But by all means, keep it in mind for the future.

That's about it for **The Beginners Guide to Investing**. Not that tough! Not that scary! Just follow the recipe and you'll be on your way to building wealth.

Subsection Six: How do I buy assets instead of liabilities?

In this chapter we are talking about things that are simple, but not easy. Well, here you go… **If you want to be rich, buy assets**! It's excellent advice, if you know how to do it. The problem is most people don't know an asset from their … Okay, I can't write that in a book to my grandchildren, but it's true.

Let me put it this way. If you ask people to list their assets, they might include their car, jewelry, clothes, smart phone, boat, timeshare or television, because they believe that an asset is something they own that is worth something or that they can turn into cash. And in every case, they would be wrong. Or they might list the cash in their checking account, their business or their home, because they believe that an asset is something that has the **potential** to make money. And in many of these cases they would also be wrong. What they should be listing are the things they own that put money in their pocket, things like interest-earning deposits, stocks, bond, passive-income businesses, rent-producing properties.

An asset is something that makes money for you! Exclamation point! Everything else you spend your resources on is a liability, meaning it costs you money. If you want to be financially secure, self-reliant, or wealthy, you should spend your resources on assets instead of liabilities. The hard part is knowing how to recognize and buy assets. Here's how you do that.

1. **Understand what liabilities are and why we buy them.**

Everything you spend money on that doesn't make money is a liability and that includes almost everything. Staying alive is a liability because you have to pay for food, shelter, clothing, utilities and medical care, but it's worth it. Having children is a liability because it costs to bring them into the world and take care of them until they launch, but it's one of the best things I've ever done. Owning a home is a liability because it's really just a big money pit, but home ownership has been very, very good to me.

However, not all liabilities serve such noble ends. For example, a brand-new car is a really dumb liability purchase. Brand-new cars are so expensive that few people can get one without borrowing money. Brand-new cars lose up to 20% of their value the moment you drive them off the lot and up to 50% the first three years you own them. "Investing" in an overpriced item, that puts you into debt, makes you pay interest and depreciates so fast you will have a hard time paying it off before it's lost most of its value, is not cool and certainly no way to get rich.

But I need reliable transportation Grandpa and I don't want to drive a beater!

Fine, stay poor! Seriously, a reliable car is an acceptable liability and you can save up to buy a nicer car.

But it's your worry about driving a beater that bothers me. This is where your desire to be financially independent comes into direct conflict with your pride (or whatever other emotion is clouding your view). It's WHY you want the brand-new car that influences you to purchase a bad liability. If you can be satisfied with a decent, well-maintained vehicle that gets you from point A to point B; if you can be wise, delay gratification, shop for a great deal on a nicer car; and pay cash; not only will you become financially independent sooner, you'll make Grandpa proud. Learn to understand the WHY behind your liability purchases.

2. Have and follow a well-devised strategy for buying liabilities.

By this time, you are probably getting sick of reading, "Have a plan! Have a plan!" so I am not going to say that. Instead, I'll say "Have a strategy! Have a strategy!" A strategy is a mini-plan that can be applied in a variety of situations, your "go-to." It's a knee jerk reaction every time you are faced with a decision.

You will develop your own strategy, or set of them, as you gain experience, but for right now, I would like you to practice developing a strategy and applying it to buying some liabilities. Take a few minutes to write down the questions you think are important to ask yourself before buying something.

I'll wait!

Now that you have your list, compare it to the list of questions below that I try to ask myself before making a liability purchase. My list will probably be different from your list because you'll have to make quite a few stupid purchases in your life before you're as smart as me. Asking yourself clarifying questions such as these, about a liability purchase, is the first step in our strategy.

- Is this a necessity or a luxury?
- WHY am I buying it?
- What is it going to cost (be sure to count **all** the costs)?
- What are at least two other less-expensive-but-acceptable ways to accomplish my WHY?

After honestly answering these questions, the next step in our strategy will be to decide how to best accomplish your WHY. You'll have three options.

- You can do it now, using your intended liability.
- You can do it now, using one of the alternatives.
- You can do it later and, instead, save the money or, better yet, invest in an asset.

If you decide to go ahead and incur a liability, your final step in the strategy will be to have a plan for buying it. Here is the simple plan we will use for this example.

- Determine how you are going to pay for it.
- Obtain at least three bids and make the providers compete.
- Avoid or manage any long-term obligations.
- Discuss the idea with at least one member of your team.
- Wait **at least** 24 hours after you've done all of the above to "ink" the deal.

Now that we have a strategy in place, let's test it.

Let's say you're a 16-year-old living at home with your parents, with a part-time job at a restaurant a mile away and you're thinking about buying a car. *Sounds like you at 16, Grandpa!* As part of this scenario think through and jot down your answers to our first set of strategy questions from above.

I'll wait!

How easy was it for you to answer these questions? I predict that you may have had some difficulty with at least a few of them. That's because you have not yet trained your mind to ask these kinds of clarifying questions about buying things. Take a minute to compare your answers to Grandpa's answers below.

- Is it a necessity or a luxury? ***Definitely a luxury.***

- WHY am I buying it? ***I need to get to work and school, but, honestly, I just want my own car.***

- What's it going to cost? ***$2500 for the car (more if I finance it). $200 upfront for title, taxes and registration, and about $100 a year for registration after that. Insurance will be about $65 a month (more if I want collision). $125 a month for upkeep and repairs. $100 a month for gas.***

- Alternatives? ***1) I already have a bike that I can ride to school and work when the weather is good. 2) I can take the bus when the weather is bad. School bus is free. UTA pass is $63 a month. 3) Mom and dad say I can use their cars when I really need one, I'll just have to pay the increase in their insurance premium and for gas and agree to clean their cars twice a month.***

Now, take a moment to decide what would be the best solution (from our options above) to accomplishing the WHY in this situation.

I'll wait some more!

My second prediction is that your best solution was to solve the problem "now, using another asset" because you really do need to get to work and school, but you don't really need a car. You see, when you honestly answer clarifying questions and consider the options, the decision is much easier and clearer. We don't even need to talk about a plan for incurring the liability of a car.

But let's suppose the circumstances are different. Let's say you are a 22-year-old married student, with a 30-mile commute to school, another 20-mile commute to your great paying job and really poor bus service in your area. Your answers to the clarifying question swill be different and since you no longer just **want** a car, but **need** one, your decision would likely be "now, with your intended liability" (i.e. buy a car). At that juncture you would move onto determining the wisest way to buy that liability. For this demonstration we'll use the buying plan outlined above. And, by the way, you should have your plan in place before you go car shopping.

First, you'll ask yourself **how you are going to pay for the car**. How much do you have in your savings bucket for a car? And what kind of car will that buy you? This is where a good WHY comes into play. If you are looking for modest, decent transportation, you'll be less likely to need a car loan. If you need a car loan, shop, shop, shop the rate and the terms. Pay as much down as you can and make the length of your loan as short as possible.

Second, you need to **have three or more vehicle options to consider**. Grandpa does not like car shopping so I cannot give you a car shopping clinic, but for people who like to car shop, this is the fun part. If someone on your team is good at this, have them help you.

> When Grandpa was young cars approaching 100,000 miles were considered to be at the end of their usefulness and it was a big deal to watch the odometer turn over from 99,999 to 100,000. Today, because of improvements in materials and design, cars can last twice or three times that (depending on the model and how well their cared for.) 100,000 miles isn't the red flag is used to be.

Third, you're going to **avoid or manage long term obligations**. Negotiate for a warrantee (and get it in writing), but avoid extended warrantees (they are a rip off). And if you have a car loan, determine how you're going to get it paid off ASAP. And remember the liability costs don't end with the purchase, you have taxes, insurance and registration; gas and oil; maintenance and repairs; parking and tolls. You should have counted all these costs before making your decision to buy, so they are not a surprise.

Fourth, make sure **you run both** the idea to buy and the details of your purchase **by a trusted and experienced member of your team**. Listen to their advice. They will most likely teach you something and may save you a lot of expense and trouble.

Last of all, **wait at least 24 hours** after you've decided which vehicle to purchase before inking the deal. If you want to know if this is an important step, just tell **any** salesman at **any** car dealership you're going to think about it and come back tomorrow and watch their reaction. They will pressure you to buy because they know that during those 24 hours you will be out from under their influence and be able to think things over clearly. And that is exactly what you want to do. If after waiting at least 24 hours, you feel good about the purchase, feel free to incur that liability.

Grandpa, this is a lot of work! Do you want me to apply this strategy to every liability purchase I ever make! Well, the answer is **yes** and **no**!

Yes! At first, using a strategy for every purchase may seem laborious or even counter-productive, but with time and practice it becomes second nature and you don't even have to think about it. And, honestly, a large percentage of your considerations will end in the early stages anyway when you decide your intended purchase is a frivolous luxury **or** that there are better alternatives. And that's because you actually gave it some thought.

No! You will not need to apply this process to every little item you buy. For example, you've already decided to keep yourself alive by buying groceries and you don't have to keep making that decision. Just manage your grocery shopping through your spending plan and save your mental energy for the non-necessities and bigger ticket items. The bigger the purchase the more important the strategy.

3. See the value of assets and have a strategy to buy them.

To help you understand how to benefit from accumulating assets, I want to share the idea of an asset **as taught by Richard Kiyosaki**. His simplistic explanation may drive your accountant crazy because it is not the textbook explanation. But I have to ask: "Who is better off financially, your accountant or Richard Kiyosaki (worth about $100 million)?" To help, I am going to use my version of the diagrams from his book, *Rich Dad, Poor Dad*. Mr. Kiyosaki suggests that one of the basics of financial literacy is understanding how money flows through our personal economies.

Before I talk about that, I want you to understand two things. One is that you should always pay the Lord first (period)! That is not pictured in Mr. Kiyosaki's diagrams below, but is certainly implied for you. The second is that everybody (rich, poor, middle class) has living expenses (rent, food, transportation, clothes and taxes) and what's left over is often called discretionary income. Wise people pay themselves that discretionary income before they pay their living expenses and they use it to buy assets.

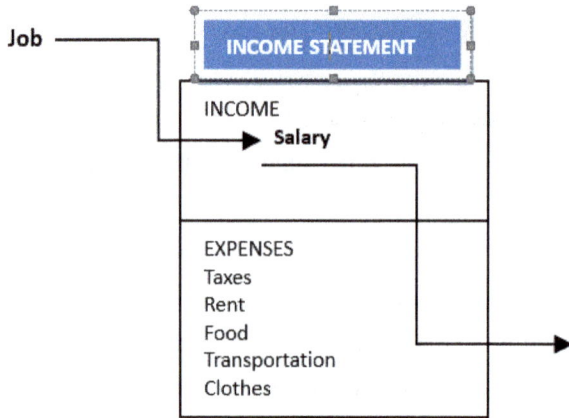

In this diagram we see the path that money takes for the **poor and people who don't manage their money.** They have a job, get paid and then spend their money on living expenses first and waste what they have left (if anything) on liabilities. In the end, they don't have anything to show for their money.

The next diagram shows how cash flows for most of the **middle class.** These are people who may have a good education, a good job, make good money, but also pay their living expenses first and spend an ever-increasing amount of their income on liabilities. In the end, they really don't have anything to show for their money but big piles of stuff they have to keep working to pay for, replenish, maintain, upgrade or store.

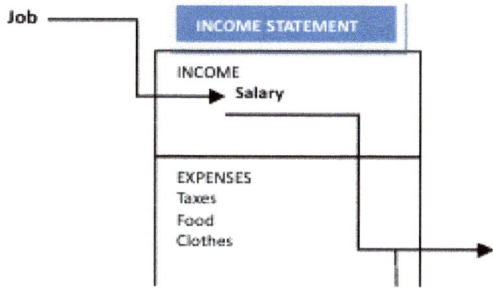

The last diagram shows the cash flow of financially literate people, the **financially independent and truly rich**. These people use their income to buy assets (that put money into their pockets) instead of liabilities. As their assets grow, their income grows (without any additional effort) and they buy even more assets. A wonderfully vicious cycle.

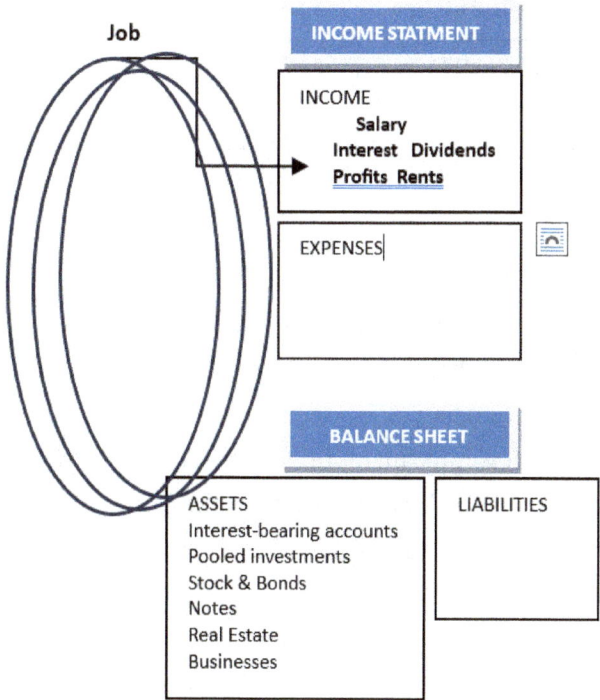

Now, these diagrams are too simple. Everybody has expenses; truly poor and truly rich people (except for FIRE Followers) will buy or maintain some type of liabilities; and many of the middle class will probably have at least some kind of asset (like a 401K). But we are looking for patterns here.

The pattern you want to see in your life is more of your income being used to buy assets that will generate more income which can be used to buy more assets which… You get the idea. Assets are investments that generate income like those we've been talking about. Forgoing or limiting liabilities in favor of investments will make financially independence and self-reliance easier and easier as time goes on.

You can easily see how forgoing the purchase of the latest I-phone and using that money to buying some Apple stock gives you an asset, but how does saving $5 by taking leftovers to work instead of going out to lunch buy you assets – after all it's only $5? The answer is that those type of choices have a cumulative effect. Transfer that $5 from your checking account to your growth CD each day of a workweek and you have a $25 asset. Do it for a month and you have a $100 asset. Do it for a year? $1250!

This is a good time to make application of one of my favorite Book of Mormon scriptures.

> Now ye may suppose that this is foolishness in me; but behold I say unto you, that by small and simple things are great things brought to pass; and small means in many instances doth confound the wise. (Alma 37:6)

I warn you that knowing about assets and wanting assets and even giving up liabilities in favor of assets are **no good unless you act**. Saved money (like the money you didn't spend on the I-phone or saved lunch money) left lying around in piles just… (Let's all say it together!) …*buys tools for the devil's workshop.* Get saved money out of your bank account and use it to buy assets. If you want that $300 share of Microsoft stock, save your lunch money for three months in a CD and buy a share when the CD matures.

4. Mitigate liabilities or turn them into assets.

> **BIG WORD WARNNG**
> **Mitigate means to make something less serious or less harmful.**

My last suggestion relating to liabilities and assets is to mitigate liabilities or turn them into assets. You do this by finding ways to make money using your liabilities.

What if you own a ski boat? You have to pay taxes on it, license it, register it, insure it, repair and maintain it, and store it. You also need a trailer and vehicle to tow it and it's no fun without all the accessories (life jackets, tubes, skis, tow rope). Without question it's a liability. But what if, when you're not using it, you rent it out to other families to use. The money you make will help mitigate the cost of owning the boat and **if you make more than it costs** you to own maintain and use the boat, you have **created an asset**.

Another example might be your pickup truck. Yes, it's a liability, but what if you used it to haul people's junk to the dump? This **does not make your pickup an asset**, because it's your labor (hauling stuff to the dump) that you're selling and assets make money for you without any additional labor. But as long as you make more money than it costs to run your pickup to the dump, you'll be **mitigating the costs** of owning your pickup.

Once you start thinking about it, the possibilities for mitigating and turning are as numerous as your liabilities. Rent out your guesthouse (or a room in your house) as a bed and breakfast. Rent out your power tools or use them to do handy-(wo)man jobs. Rent out storage space in your garage or let people park their trailer on you RV pad. Use your bicycle to deliver packages. Now there are logistics to all of this, so you'll have to decide if it is worth the hassle. But over the last several years, all kinds of companies have sprung up to help people do this kind of thing. It's amazing how they help providers work through it all.

Remember these points. If you are using a liability to do a job, it's a job not an asset, but that job can offset the cost of the liability. Your liability costs might be more than you make, but you're still offsetting the cost of the liability. If you make more than it costs to own and maintain the asset, and don't do any additional work, you've turned a liability into an asset. And any money earned only becomes an asset when it … (you've got it) … is used to buy assets.

Now, before we leave the subject, I have a few thoughts about liabilities and assets. I may have set you up to feel some guilt for owning liabilities. That's good if it helps you buy more assets instead, but, just like money, liabilities are neither good nor bad. It's WHY you own them, what you do with them and how seriously they keep you from becoming secure and self-reliant that makes them good or bad.

Uncle John and Aunt Celeste own a ski boat. It provides their family with hours of quality family time each summer. Without question, that ski boat is a liability, but because of the way they procured it, care for it and fit it into their lifestyle, I believe it is a **reasonable and wise** liability for **them** to own.

The largest liability purchase you'll buy in your life will most likely be your own home. When the circumstances are right and you are in the financial position to do so, buying your own home is one of the wisest moves you can make. It can give you control, housing security and can build wealth through appreciation. It should fit your needs and be modest. You need to maintain it, improve it and work to pay the mortgage down so you have equity and security. Buying your own home is the one and only time I would ever agree with stretching *a* **little** financially to obtain a liability.

One of the most successful investors of the last two centuries, Warren Buffet (worth $142 billion) still lives a modest home in the suburbs of Omaha, Nebraska that he bought for $31,500 in 1958.

Chapter 7: How Do I Protect What I Have and Love

I've heard them all my life!

Better safe than sorry!

A stitch, in time, saves nine!

An ounce of prevention is worth a pound of cure!

Look before you leap!

A prudent man foreseeth the evil, and hideth himself... (Proverbs 22:3)

All of these old-school sayings speak to the virtue I am about to teach you. As a good steward, you have the responsibility to protect the things (and people) that you love. There are few things that Grandpa actually hates, but he does hate waste and ingratitude. And not protecting what God has given you is wastefulness and ingratitude.

Protecting the things and people you love is a very, very broad subject – almost worthy of its own book. We, however, are dealing with financial things in this book so our discussion will be much narrower, but even then... Well, you better buckle up!

1. A stich, in time, saves nine.

Over 50 years ago, I saw a TV commercial for Fram oil filters. A mechanic extolled the virtue of changing your car's oil filter regularly to prevent damage. His catch phrase was, "you can pay me now ($4 oil filter) or pay me later ($200 bearing replacement)". That message must have hit home because Fram used different versions of that commercial for the next 20 years. Everything you own is destined to fall apart, quit working or waste away. You cannot totally keep this from happening, but you can delay the process – sometimes for a very, very long time.

> It's called a sinking fund because in the 1700's the British government set aside money each year to pay off (or sink) their national debt. Today it refers to saving up money to fund for a future purchase or obligation.

This is called upkeep and maintenance. It costs time and money, but if you do it, your "stuff" will last much longer. If you don't, you will either lose what you have or have to pay more to restore or replace it. Your spending plan should include buckets for upkeep and maintenance as well as a **sinking fund** to replace items that do eventually wear out, but if you will develop good habits for taking care of your belongings and follow a maintenance schedule, you'll be less likely to have to spend that money.

Remember you can pay now or pay later!

2. An ounce of prevention is worth a pound of cure.

While we don't have the power to eliminate loss, we can reduce the risk. That is called prevention. If you keep your car in good repair and drive safely, you'll be less likely to be involved in a costly accident. If you remove flammables from your house and keep matches out of the reach of little children, your house is less likely to burn down. If your yard is secure and well lit, you'll lose much less to theft. Again, prevention costs time and money and requires some organization, but it's smart and will save you grief and expense in the long run.

3. An apple a day keeps the doctor away.

The advice offered in the paragraphs above applies to everything that God has loaned to you, including your body. Most of the things you own can, with enough money, be replaced, but **your body is not one of them**. Illness, injury and death are part of the plan. They teach us appreciation, patience, faith and empathy. But, just like all other forms of loss we can reduce health risk with healthy habits. And unlike other forms of prevention, upkeep and maintenance, healthy habits are almost free.

Developing healthy habits early in life and continuing them into old age is one of the smartest moves you can make. When you're young, your body is much more forgiving. It can compensate and heal more quickly from abuse, illness and injury. As you age, your body gets tired of the abuse and neglect and begins to balk. When you are old, it yells "Enough!"

What does health have to do with money? Being unhealthy is very, very expensive. Not only are medical costs expensive, but they're getting more expensive all the time and the cost of treating serious illness is astronomical. As a matter of fact, unpaid medical bills are the most frequent cause of bankruptcy. And as you get older and your body begins to wear out, medical cost can become even more expensive.

> **Bankruptcy is a legal action that people and businesses can take when they have so much debt, they cannot possibly pay it off. If granted, a bankruptcy can free you from some of your debts and protect some of your assets from creditors. It can, however, play havoc with your financial reputation and is often seen as a last resort.**

4. A prudent man forseeth the evil and hideth himself.

> **Hedging your bet means to reduce your risk by arranging for multiple possibilities or making counterbalancing moves.**

Upkeep, maintenance and prevention are essential, but even with your best efforts, bad things can and will happen. If you are wise, you will hedge your bet when it comes to loss. This is where insurance comes in. When you buy insurance, you are basically making a bet with an insurance company. You are betting that you will incur a loss and they are betting that you won't. If **you** are right, they pay to restore all or part of your loss. If **they** are right, they get to keep your money. This is one of the few bets you really want to lose.

Insurance companies will insure most anything (for the right price), but some types of insurance are more vital or give you greater value than others. Insurance is vital when it's required (by law or policy) or when it's foolish to forego. Most states require that you carry a certain amount of insurance to operate a car – if you're caught driving a car without it, they will actually suspend your driver's license. When you take out a mortgage, the mortgage company requires you to keep homeowners' insurance on the house – if not, they will put a policy on it themselves and make you pay for it. Both of these insurances are required, but even if they weren't you'd be stupid not to have them. If you cause a wreck, you certainly want money to pay medical bills and property damage. If your house burns down, you certainly want money to rebuild your house and replace your belongings.

Other forms of insurance that Grandpa sees as vital include medical and life insurance. Catastrophic medical insurance pays part or all of your medical bills if you have a serious medical emergency. Without this kind of coverage, you may be tempted to forego important medical procedures or, more likely, go into debilitating debt to obtain them. If you have a spouse or children, you need life insurance. This type of insurance pays your surviving family money to help them carry on if you die; without it, you could leave your family in serious financial trouble.

There are generally two reasons why people **don't** buy insurance. Either they are ignorant about insurance or they think it's too expensive. As a good steward, you definitely should educate yourself about the various forms of insurance, how they work and what they cost. Sometimes they are not worth the price, but other times they are a screaming deal. Let's take a few minutes to consider some of the logistics of insurance.

First of all, let's talk about **how insurance works**. The "job" of insurance is to transfer the financial risk from customers to the insurance company – if a customer has a loss, the insurance company will make all or part of it up. When customers buy insurance from a company, the money goes into an account (and is invested in very safe investments) until it is needed to reimburse one of the customers for a loss. The more people that buy insurance from a company, the more money there is in the account; and the fewer claims customers make, the more that account grows. The insurance company takes its expenses and profits out of the account.

If well run (and lucky) an insurance company can make a lot of money, if poorly managed (or there are too many claims) an insurance company can lose money. Because insurance companies affect so many people's lives, in such a big way, they are heavily regulated by state governments and backed up by guaranty associations.

Secondly, let's talk about the **different kinds of insurance**. You can insure almost anything from your Altima (car insurance) to your zebra (pet insurance), but the types of personal insurance you will usually deal with fall into the following categories.

- Property and Casualty insurance protects you from loss due to the damage to or loss of your stuff (e.g. home, car, belongings).

- Life insurance protects your family from loss of income due to your death.
- Liability insurance protects you when you're responsible for damages and injuries.
- Health insurance provides coverage for medical costs.
- Disability insurance provides you an income if you become unable to work.

Next, **let's talk about cost**. Insurance companies provide a great service, but they are in the business of making money. There are A LOT of insurance companies out there competing and this keeps the costs down, but they are still in the business of making money. So, to make sure they charge customers enough to cover the cost of any loss they may incur and still make money, insurance companies hire people who are really good at statistics (called actuaries) and have them figure out the odds of you getting in a wreck, having your house burn down or dying and they set their prices accordingly. Once they have set their prices, they must report them to the state government and stick with them for a set period of time. So, you will NEVER see insurance go on sale!

Wait, grandpa! My dad says when I get my driver's license his car insurance rates are going to go way up.

Yeah, and my dad says he got in an accident and his rates went up.

And my dad says if he doesn't get a speeding ticket his rates will do down.

Enough already!! Your dads are all correct, but not for the reasons you are thinking.

Part of the price setting that actuaries do involves manipulating all kinds of data and putting people and property into all kinds of categories that affect the rates they charge. 16-year-old male drivers are much more likely to get in a car wreck than any other group of drivers and actuaries will charge more to insure them. Yesterday you were 15 and your dad was enjoying a pretty good rate because 35 to 59-year-old, married guys with dad bods have fewer accidents, but today you started to drive and his rates went way up. Not fair, you say? Unfortunately for you at 16, it's totally fair. Newer cars cost more to insure because they cost more to replace. Homes with smoke detectors and dead-bolt locks are less likely to burn down or get robbed, so they get a discount. And who do you think get the best price on life insurance, an out of shape 60-year-old or a healthy 18-year-old? It's totally fair.

And to make it **even more fair**, rates are often set based on behaviors that affect risk. Get in a car wreck or get your license suspended and your rates go up. Don't get a speeding ticket and don't have a wreck and your rates go down. Lose 50 pounds and stop smoking and you can buy a cheaper life insurance policy. Install an alarm system on your house and your insurance company may reduce your rates.

And to make it **even more and more fair**, where you live may make a difference in your rates. If you live in a high crime area; or if the roads around you home are in poor condition; or if your house is too far away from a fire station; you may have to pay more for insurance – if you can get it. Right now, people in parts of California cannot even buy fire insurance because of the increase in wildfires.

Every insurance company has its own set of rules. Some may have better rates for one type of insurance and poorer rates for others. Some may give you a loyalty discount for

> One of the reasons Grandpa loves his insurance company is that when he rents a car for a trip, his insurer lets Grandpa call up and change the deductibles (more on those below) on his insurance to better cover the rental car. Then when he is back home, he calls them up and changes it back. This saves Grandpa a good chunk of change and whenever I shop rates, I ask about this benefit. By the way, Grandpa has been with the same auto insurer for over 50 years.

having more than one insurance policy with them. Some may give you discount for being a good driver. And every insurance company will offer you a different level of service, which may be even more important than cost. So, it's important to shop and compare rates and service often.

You can use deductibles to reduce insurance costs. If you are willing to assume the first $1000 or $2000 of risk in case you get in an auto accident, your auto insurance will be cheaper than if the insurance company assumes all the risk. It's the same with health insurance, the more in medical cost risk you are willing to assume the lower your monthly premiums will be.

My final counsel about cost is what I call the **catsup principle**. You can buy a 14 oz bottle of catsup for about $3 (21.4 cents per ounce) or a 114 oz bottle for about $12 (10.5 cents per ounce). It's the same with insurance. The most expensive part of insurance is the minimum amount, once you have met the base level, insurance gets relatively cheaper. In certain cases, this may make beefing up your insurance a good idea.

Finally, let's talk **about how much insurance you "need"**. Grandpa considers it foolish to go without adequate insurance, but you **can** waste money on insurance. Like I said before, some insurances are required, but for insurances (or levels of insurance) that are optional, you need to do some critical thinking.

For example, if you drive a $1000 car, you need liability insurance, but it doesn't make much sense to pay a $80 a month for collision coverage (that pays to fix your car if it's in a wreck). You will pay more for collision insurance in just over a year than the car is worth and your chances of totally wrecking that beater are pretty slim. You'd be better off putting that $80 away each month in a car-repair/replacement savings bucket.

On the other hand, make sure you are not underinsured. Let's suppose you just carry the minimum liability on your car (currently $25,000 bodily injury / $15,000 property damage in Utah). You cause a wreck which results in a $80,000 loss ($50,000 in medical bills and $30,000 to replace a car). Your insurance company will pay the first $25,000 in medical bills and $15,000 toward replacing the other driver's car, but who pays the other $40,000? That's right, you can be sued for those expenses. It does not cost that much more to carry $50,000/$30,000 in coverage because of the catsup principle. Just carrying the minimum is often the least cost-effective option in the long run.

Grandpa could go on and on and on about insurance, but I will conclude with some final thoughts on insurance.

- Medical insurance is a very important part of a wise protection plan. If your employer does not offer you a good plan, you can buy a personal plan. Between the Affordable Care Act, state market places and high-deductible plans everyone can now afford coverage, so don't ever go without.

- Whole life and term life insure exactly what they say. Whole life insures you for your whole life but costs a lot more. Term life only insures you for the term that you pay the premiums, but it's way cheaper. Once you no longer need to leave your dependents money to live on after you die, you don't need life insurance. This makes whole life a waste.

- Often your employer will offer you a very affordable term life policy as a benefit and it might be a good way to beef up your coverage while you need it, but you should always have your own term life policy in place in case you lose your employee coverage.

- Insurance is a great tool for transferring risk, but it's a mediocre tool for investment. Whole life is often sold as a way to build up a cash reserve as an investment **or** as a fund to borrow from. But because it costs so much more that term, you're better off taking that extra money and just investing it.

- Extended warrantees and home maintenance plans are not insurance policies and are usually not a good deal. In the long run you'll do better with a repair/replace savings bucket.

- Identity theft is a real problem and you need to protect your identification and reputation. There are many things you can do to prevent identity theft, but it's also a good idea to have a policy that will help reimburse you for financial loss and help restore your reputation.

- Grandpa is a fan of umbrella policies – a policy that covers you with beefed up liability insurance. If you have the right coverages on your home and auto, you can get a $1,000,000 or $2,000,000 of extra coverage for a few hundred dollars a year. This is a great example of the catsup principle.

"Be a man, my son". One of Grandpa's favorite poems is *If* by Rudyard Kipling. I've included it below and hope you'll take the time to read it. It's a powerful word painting of the kind of man that every father wants his child to be. (I know it says son/man, but it applies to daughter/woman too.) If I were to reduce this poem to just one word, I would use the word **character**, to mean "the mental and moral characteristics of an individual" (Oxford Dictionary).

Near the top of all the things you want to protect should be your character and reputation. Phony or exaggerated reputations have no place on the list. Protect the "you" that is true to your nature, pure in motive, integrous in both public and private; and competent in what you do.

You will ultimately decide what you want your character to include, but being a life-long Scouter, I am partial to the set of values in the Scout Law – trustworthy, loyal, helpful, friendly, courteous, kind, obedient, cheerful, thrifty, brave, clean and reverent. When Benjamin Franklin was a young man, he embarked on a "project of moral perfection" and came up with a list of 13 values he would work on for the rest of his life. I suggest you take some time to seriously think about what kind of a person you want to be and write it down. Once you've decided what you want to be and start working on it, do all you can to cultivate, maintain and protect both your character and reputation.

But Grandpa, what does this have to do with money? This has a lot to do with money. It is the reason you'll be trusted and invested in. It can be leveraged for aid and assistance. It will allow you to build an empire and a kingdom. It will serve you better than all the lawyers, counselors, accountants and employees combined.

If –

By Rudyard Kipling

If you can keep your head when all about you
    Are losing theirs and blaming it on you,
If you can trust yourself when all men doubt you,
    But make allowance for their doubting too;
If you can wait and not be tired by waiting,
    Or being lied about, don't deal in lies,
Or being hated, don't give way to hating,
    And yet don't look too good, nor talk too wise:

If you can dream—and not make dreams your master;
    If you can think—and not make thoughts your aim;
If you can meet with Triumph and Disaster
    And treat those two impostors just the same;
If you can bear to hear the truth you've spoken
    Twisted by knaves to make a trap for fools,
Or watch the things you gave your life to, broken,
    And stoop and build 'em up with worn-out tools:

If you can make one heap of all your winnings
    And risk it on one turn of pitch-and-toss,
And lose, and start again at your beginnings
    And never breathe a word about your loss;
If you can force your heart and nerve and sinew
    To serve your turn long after they are gone,
And so hold on when there is nothing in you
    Except the Will which says to them: 'Hold on!'

If you can talk with crowds and keep your virtue,
    Or walk with Kings—nor lose the common touch,
If neither foes nor loving friends can hurt you,
    If all men count with you, but none too much;
If you can fill the unforgiving minute
    With sixty seconds' worth of distance run,
Yours is the Earth and everything that's in it,
    And—which is more—you'll be a Man, my son!

Chapter 8: How Can I Be Generous with My Riches?

I saved my most heartfelt counsel for this last chapter – not because it is the last thing you should do, but because I want it to be the last thing I impress upon your mind. It also fits well at the end of a book about money because after you've mastered all the advice given in the book, you'll be better prepared to be generous. Remember one of the purposes of self-reliance is to lift others and help them become self-reliant.

To provide a framework for this subject, let's suppose that as you are driving out of the Walmart parking lot one morning, you see a dirty and disheveled guy sitting on the curb with a sign that says, "Homeless and Hungry: Please Help!" Close your eyes and see this guy in your mind's eye for a moment, then come back and do the following.

Ask yourself what you **could** do.

Ask yourself what you **should** do.

Then ask yourself, honestly, what you **would** do.

Is your answer to all three questions the same? Why or why not?

I use this image because it's about as awkward as it gets for most of you. You hate the idea that he is suffering or in need, but you also don't want to enable his bad decisions, throw your money away on drugs or booze, or be his patsy. You know that if you can avoid eye contact for just a few moments you can be on your way and forget about him. The problem is, he (or one of his peers) will be here next time, and the next time and if you helped every guy holding a sign, you'd go broke. Okay, maybe your thought process is a **little** different, but I'm betting that it makes you uncomfortable to some level.

I propose that your levels of comfort or discomfort, guilt or innocence, action or inaction, really have to do with your answers to the three questions posed above. Let's talk about each of them. As we do, **don't limit your thinking to the guy at Walmart**. Think more broadly about all the kinds of opportunities you have to help your fellow man.

What could you do? You might be tempted to limit yourself by how much cash you have in your pocket at the moment, but handing him your "spare change" is only one option. Your options actually range from ignoring him to selling everything you own, cleaning out your bank account and giving it all to him. (Then you would need your own sign.) Somewhere in the huge list of things you could do are a few close-to-perfect responses for that person, at that moment, using your available resources. In order to know what those near-perfects responses might be you need to move on to the next question.

What should you do? The answer to this question really flows out of your motivations. If you are motivated by intolerance, guilt or greed, your answer will be very different than if your motivations are love and gratitude. If you truly love this fellow man, you will want to do what you can to **best** help him. That may be doing something, right then, to relieve his suffering, (hand him a couple of bucks, buy him a meal, take a few moments to talk with him) or not (allow him to hit rock bottom so he'll get real help, make a donation to homeless relief efforts when you get home, not enable his addictions). If you are truly grateful for all that God has done for you, you'll be less judgmental and more likely to do something.

You will be limited by what you can afford to do, what is safe for you to do, what you have time to do. If you **really** don't have the money, feel safe or have the time, but would if you did, at least King Benjamin would give you a pass (see Mosiah 4:24-25). But King Benjamin would expect you to be honest about this and do what is right.

So how do you know what is right? Well, I have two suggestions that will help you know. The first is to be in tune with the Holy Ghost and act upon his promptings. I can't tell you how that will feel – you have your own relationship with the Holy Ghost and he speaks to you in a different way than he does to me, but I can tell you, in general, that it's likely to be a feeling of peace, confidence and courage. The second is to be proactive. Often, we aren't sure what to do because we are caught off guard, but if you are actively thinking, preparing and serving, the right things will be second nature and you'll be ready to act.

What would (will) you really do? I hope your answer to this question is that you will do the right thing. End of story! But to bring it all back to money, I think it's important to realize that having more money will **not** make you generous. Generosity is a matter of character demonstrated by the poor and the rich. You either choose (or learn) to be generous or not. However, more money will give you the **option** to be more generous. It will give you the **free time** that you may choose to use to help others. It will bring you into **contact with other good, well-off people** who you can synergize with to do wonderful things.

You can be generous today! As far as I know, no person ever went broke being too generous. Take advantage of opportunities, organizations and programs that allow you to be generous. Do this with your **limited** means until you get to the point where you can do more. In the last part of his address to the Nephites, King Benjamin taught about being Christ-like after we are born again. Part of his teachings (Mosiah 4:13-28), springs to mind whenever I think about parting with my riches to help others. In a nutshell, I believe King Benjamin is saying that you should…

…live in peace with your fellow man and treat them fairly. (v.13)

…provide for, teach and take care of your own family. (v.14)

…use what you have to help those that stand in need. (v. 16)

…not judge or withhold help from someone because you think they've brought neediness or misery upon themselves. We are all beggars before God for everything from our daily needs to forgiveness for our sins. (v. 17-22)

...carry the desire in our hearts to help others and do the best we can depending on our circumstance (vv. 23-26)

...use wisdom in giving to the needy (v. 27).

My personal counsel to you is simple. When it comes to helping others, be motivated by love for them and not by guilt. If you really love someone, you will try to help them in ways that help them become self-reliant and maintain their dignity. And remember that riches include so much more than just money. Riches include time, effort, opportunity and education. Think about how you can share these non-monetary riches with those in need.

Appendix A: 101 Gigs, Side-hustles and Businesses for Youth

Service Businesses

- Babysitting
- Mother's helper
- After-school care
- Pet sitting
- Dog walking
- Dog training
- Poop removal
- House/Plant sitting
- Landscaping (mowing, weeding, raking leaves)
- Snow removal
- Patriotic flag business
- House cleaning
- Window washing
- Gutter cleaning
- Gift wrapping
- Errand running
- Personal shopping
- Personal delivery service
- House painting
- Pressure washing (trash cans, driveways, houses)
- Window washing

- Cars washing and detailing
- Laundry service
- Sewing new and repairs
- Handyman service
- Photography
  - Family
  - Newborn
  - Engagement or wedding
  - Real estate
  - Senior pictures
  - Missionary
- Tutoring (math, science, language)
- Musical performance
- Music Lessons
- Party planning
- Summer camps for kids
- Website design
- Christmas décor put up / take down
- Yard Selling
- Yard Sale Organization / Consignment
- Roof cleaning
- Junk removal business
- Recycle metal
- Sneaker cleaning / Reselling sneakers

- Bike repair / Bike repair clinics for kids
- Trash can service (putting them out, bringing them in)
- Flat tire and bicycle repair

Produce and Sell (Online stores / Roadside stands / Fairs / Markets / Door to door)

- Fruits and vegetables
- Flowers / vegetable starts
- Chickens and eggs
- Bees and Honey
- Crafts / Artwork
- Books / E-books
- Candles
- Soaps
- Bakery goods/ cakes
- Dog biscuits / treats
- Apps / games
- Downloadable digital products
- Golf balls collected from course traps.
- Print-on-demand projects
  - Books
  - Apparel (t-shirts, hats, onesies)
  - Mugs
  - Bags / Backpack
  - Stickers / Bumper stickers
- Refurbished furniture
- Flipping business (clothes, furniture, antiques)
- Curate / Organize craft fairs / pop-up markets

Online and Computer Based Businesses

- Bogging

- Podcasting
- YouTube channel
- Graphic art design
- Help older generation with technology
- Create online content
- Video editing and production
- Designing YouTube thumbnails
- Social media management
- Retelling history / scripture stories
- Product review / Associate marketing / Influencing
- Skills Instruction
  - How to fix flats and repair bicycles
  - Coding
  - Language
  - Photography / Photoshop
  - Personal finance for kids
  - Microsoft products (Xcel, Word, PowerPoint, etc.)
- Tic Toc Shopping Videos

Side Gigs

- Deliver stuff with your bike or car (pizza, Uber Eats, Amazon Flex, Spark)
- Testing apps, websites and games
- Doing online surveys
- Mystery Shopping
- Wait in line for other people
- Referee a sport
- Donate plasma
- Do transcription
- Proofread
- Data entry

Appendix B: Sneaky Fees and Interest Details in the Loan Business

If you've ever squeezed a fresh, juicy lemon and wanted to get every drop of sour juiciness from it, you will know how lenders feel. Lenders pretend to be doing you a big favor when they loan you money (and sometimes they can be helpful), but their most important reason for existing is to make as much money off of you as they possibly can. And they are good at it. I have listed in this appendix 1) examples of the kind of sneaky fees lenders use to make money from borrowers and 2) examples of different types of loans and their terms. Please note these are just a few of the ways lenders try to squeeze your wallet like a ripe lemon.

FEES

Overdraft fees – this is the fee you pay if you overdraw your bank account. Banks and credit unions charge between $10 and $40 dollars for an overdraft and may charge you for each transaction or each day you are overdrawn.

Credit card use fees – the fee that credit card companies charge vendors (usually 2 to 3 %) sometimes passed on to you to encourage you to pay cash.

Credit card annual fee – some premium credit cards charge you an annual fee for just carrying their card – whether you use it or not. It can range from $25 to $500.

Late fees – lenders will charge you a fee for not making your scheduled payment on time. For credit cards this can range from $25 to $40; for a mortgage it is typically 3 to 6% of the amount you owe.

Balance transfer fee – the amount you pay to transfer debt from one credit card to another (perhaps for a better rate, better terms or some kind of reward). Usually, 3 to 5% of the transferred amount.

Over the limit fee – changed when you exceed the credit limit on your credit card --up to $35. Some companies may even charge you for calling and getting your fee increased before you spend.

Card replacement fee – charged for replacing a lost or stolen credit card. Not all companies do this, but some charge $5 to $25.

Inactivity fee – decide to not use your card for a year? The credit card company may charge you a $25 to $50 fee.

Reward redemption fee – your credit card company may charge you up to $25 for cashing in the points or miles you have earned.

Cash advance fee – use your credit card to get some cash and you may have to pay 3 to 5% of the amount you borrow with a $5 to $10 minimum.

Loan origination fees – lenders may charge you for taking your application and processing it. Usually, it is .5% to 1% of the loan amount, but they often add other smaller fees (processing, underwriting fees, etc.) They can actually add any fee they disclose and get you to agree on. Often these fees are just rolled in into your mortgage and you pay interest on them for the next 30 years.

Points – In mortgage lending, you can buy your interest rate down on some loans by paying points (1% of the loan amount).

LOAN TYPES AND TERMS

Type: New Car Loan

Security: New to practically new car

Price of Money: Fed Benchmark rate 4.5%

Interest Rate on Loan: 6%

(This loan is secured by a new car so, if you default, the bank can repossess your new car and sell it to get some of their money back. The bank pays the Federal Reserve or depositors about 4 to 5% (for the use of their money) and charge you about 6% -- making 1.5%.

Type: Credit Card Purchases

Security: You reputation

Price of Money: Depends on the credit card. The money may come from investors, banks or the Fed at various rates.

Interest Rate on Purchases: Average is 20.5%

(In this example the loan is unsecured. If you don't pay it back the credit card company will have to sue you and that is expensive. So, they take the Prime Rate (about 7.5%) and add a healthy 12 to 20% margin and make a lot of money for their "trouble.

Type: Payday Loan

Security: Temporary access to your bank account or a post-dated check.

Price of money: Usually from investors who own the business.

Interest Rate: Very high. Averages around 400% (not a typo).

(In this example lenders are taking advantage of people who need money right way. The term on these loans is usually shorter than 30 days, so the amount you are asked to pay back does not seem that much. If you borrow $500 to make your car payment and buy some food and then pay it back in two weeks you will only be charged $38 in interest – doesn't sound too bad, but that's 400% annually.)

Type: Primary Home Mortgage

Security: You home.

Price of money: Based on the 10-year U.S. Treasury bond, about 4.5%.

Interest Rate: About 6.5 to 7%

(In this example the loan is highly secured, by your home. This is one of the safest loans to make because real estate traditionally has appreciated about 2%, so the longer the mortgage is held the more secure the loan becomes.)

Glossary of LDS-Centric Terms

Grandpa is a life-long member of the Church of Jesus Christ of Latter-day Saints (sometimes called Mormon or LDS Church). So are most of my grandchildren. My use of LDS-centric terms and scripture references are second nature to me and most of my family. But, my publisher suggests, there may be others who read this book who may not be "in the know" and in that case definitions of the LDS terms used in this book might make it more readable and enjoyable. This glossary is Grandpa's attempt to do that.

I will begin with a description of The Book of Momon and then define the other unique terms in alphabetically order. I hope this helps. By the way, if you want to know more visit the Church's website at churchofjesuschrist.org or find a "Mormon" (who will be happy to tell you all about us).

The Book of Mormon – A book of ancient scripture comparable to the Bible. It tells the religious history of **some** of the ancient inhabitants of the Americas. Latter-day Saints (see Church, The) consider it to be a companion to the Bible in testifying of the divinity of Jesus Christ.

Alma – (Lived 126 – 73 BC.) There are two men named Alma in the Book of Mormon (see The Book of Mormon). The one referenced in GBBM was a leader and prophet of the Nephite people (see Nephites). He had a powerful Saul-on-the-road-to-Damacus conversion experience (see Acts 9:1-9 in the Holy Bible) that helped make him one of the most powerful prophets in the Book of Mormon (see Book of Mormon).

Alma, Book of – A section in the Book of Mormon that covers the period of time from 91 B.C. to 52 B.C. It includes historical narrative and some of the most powerful sermons and teachings about Jesus Christ in the book.

Benjamin, King – (Died about 124 B.C.) A prophet-king of the Nephites (see Nephites) who set the example of servant leadership. In his final sermon to his people, spoken from a tall tower, he taught his people about spiritual rebirth through Jesus Christ, the importance of covenants and service to our fellow man.

Bishop – A priesthood office and calling in the Church (see Church, The), similar to a pastor in other Christian faiths. A bishop is the presiding priesthood authority in a ward (see Ward) and is especially charged with guiding the youth and providing temporal guidance and assistance to ward members. He administrates the Church's Welfare programs in his ward (see Church Welfare Plan / Project(s)).

Bishopric – A group of three leaders that work together to lead an LDS ward (see Church, The; see Ward). They are led by the ward bishop (see Bishop). The two other leaders are called counselors. Each of the three leaders has a specific area of responsibility in ward leadership and administration.

BYU Pathway Worldwide – This is an educational program that provides affordable, spiritually based, and flexible higher education completely online to students in over 180 countries. It is available to all adults regardless of their religious affiliation. To learn more visit byupathway.edu.

Church Educational System – The LDS Church (see Church, The) has a worldwide educational program that provides both religious and secular education at all levels. It is called the Church Educational System (CES). Grandpa was employed by CES for 21 years as a classroom teacher and administrator on both the secondary and college level. Since his retirement he has worked as a BYU Pathway Worldwide missionary and is currently teaching online CES classes to students in Africa.

Church Self-reliance Services -- A Church (see Church, The) program designed to help members (and interested others) become more self-reliant by providing free courses, resources, and mentoring in areas like education, employment, and finances. These services combine spiritual principles and practical skills.

Church, The – The Church of Jesus Christ of Latter-day Saints is a Christian church that was organized in 1830 in New York State with six members and today has a worldwide membership of almost 18 million. Its members are often called Latter-day Saints (LDS for short) or by the nickname Mormons. Latter-day Saints often refer to their church as simply The Church (especially when talking to other members.)

Church Website – The official website of the Church of Jesus Christ of Latter-day Saints is churchofjesuschrist.org. There you can find information about the Church's beliefs and ministry. It is a wonderful (and accurate) source of information.

Church Welfare Plan / Project(s) – During the Great Depression (1930's) LDS Church (see Church, The) congregations established a series of enterprises intended to promote self-reliance. They gave members (and others) the opportunity to work and do service. Those receiving assistance would not be "on the dole", but could work in the system to develop independence and self-respect. These projects were all consolidated into the Church Welfare Plan which survived the Depression and continues today in a grand and glorious fashion. When grandpa was a boy our welfare project was a large sugar beet farm on the west side of Utah Lake where he volunteered many hours hoeing (weeding) row and rows of sugar beets in the summer.

D&C – The prophet Joseph Smith (1805-1844) and prophets who followed him have received many revelations from God for the purposes of establishing the Church (see Church, The); clarifying doctrine; answering logistical questions; and warning the world of coming calamities. Many of these revelations have been canonized in a book of scripture called the Doctrine and Covenants or the D&C (for short).

David O. McKay – (Lived 1873 to 1970.) Professional educator who later served as president of the Church of Jesus Christ of Latter-day Saints from 1952 to 1970. His grandfatherly image helped make him one of the most beloved leaders of the Church (see Church, The).

Dispensation – Seven periods in the history of the world when God has revealed his word through a new prophet and reestablished his covenant with a chosen people. The chosen prophet is referred to as the head of that dispensation. These prophets were Adam, Enoch, Noah, Abraham, Moses, Jesus Christ and Joseph Smith.

General Conference – Every six months The Church (see Church, The) holds a church-wide conference for all members. It covers several days and has sessions and trainings for different sets of leaders. The general church membership meets in four 2-hour "general" sessions over two days where they are instructed by the leaders of the Church. These meetings, collectively, are called General Conference.

Handbook 2 – The Church (see Church, The) publishes a correlated set of standards and instructions for leaders to use to teach and lead the members. These handbooks come in two volumes. Handbook 1 is for the top leaders in congregations and Handbook 2 is for all other leaders.

Helaman – There are several men named Helaman in The Book of Mormon (see The Book of Mormon). The one referenced in GBBM is Helaman, the eldest son of the prophet Alma (see Alma). We do not know when he was born, but he died in 57 B.C. He was tutored by his father and succeeded him as the leader of the Church. He was a great prophet in his own right as well as a great military leader and record keeper.

Jacob – (Lived 592 – 544 B.C.) A very early Nephite prophet. He succeeded his brother Nephi (see Nephi) as spiritual leader and felt a great responsibility to make sure his people understood the commandments of God and how to live them. He delivered a great sermon to the Nephites in which he decried immorality, greed and worldliness.

Lamanites -- A major part of Book of Mormon history centers around two related, but warring, groups of ancient Americans. (also see Nephites.) One of those groups was called the Lamanites after their common ancestor Laman. The Lamanites spend most of the story living in ignorance, wickedness and trying to destroy the Nephites. Eventually they are converted to Christ by some courageous and powerful missionaries and, for a time, their faithfulness outshines that of the Nephites.

Living Prophet(s) – A prophet is a person who has the knowledge and authority to speak for God. The Bible is filled with stories and teaching of ancient prophets. Latter-day Saints believe that in our day the Church (see Church, The) is led by prophets who have been commissioned by Jesus Christ to speak for Him and direct the affairs of His Church. They are called living prophets to distinguish them from ancient, Biblical prophets.

Mission, Missionary, Missionaries – The LDS Church (see Church, The) sends missionaries (currently about 85,000) out to love, serve, teach and baptize. They serve in over 150 nations of the world. Most are young single adults (18-25), but there are also senior single and married adults who serve. Missionary service is an expectation for young men, but young women and older missionaries are invited and welcomed to serve if they feel the call. In LDS culture being a returned missionary is considered a badge of honor and returned missionaries often refer to "my mission" or "the mission" as a time of great personal and spiritual growth.

Mosiah, Book of – A section of the Book of Mormon that cover the period of time from 130 B.C to 91 B.C., with a historical flashback to about 200 B.C. It contains historical narrative and religious teachings including King Benjamin's (see Benjamin, King) powerful sermon on being born again in Christ.

Mosiah, King – (Lived about 124 to 91 B.C.) There are two King Mosiah's in the Book of Mormon. The one referenced in GBBM is King Mosiah II, the son of King Benjamin (see, Benjamin, King). He followed in his father's footsteps as a righteous and powerful king. He had four sons who rebelled against God, but later had a marvelous conversion experience and became powerful missionaries (see Mosiah, Sons of). Inspired by God, he granted his sons' desire to go preach Jesus Christ to the Lamanites (see, Lamanite).

Mosiah, Sons of – These are the four sons of the Nephite King Mosiah II (see Nephites; see Mosiah, King) who had a dramatic conversation to Jesus Christ after having spent much of their youth trying to destroy His church. Their conversion was so powerful that they spent the rest of their lives as missionaries. They eventually went to preach to the Lamanites (see Lamanites) and converted thousands of them to Christ.

Nephi – The "father" of the Nephite nation. He was instrumental in helping his father's family escape the destruction of Jerusalem and journey to the Americas. This happened around 600 B.C. After arriving in the Americas, his father's family split (see Lamanites; see Nephites) and Nephi led the righteous to safety and in building a great society. He was a great prophet, teacher, leader and defender, but he refused to be a king, preferring servant leadership. For many generations after his death the leader of the Nephites took on the title of Nephi.

Nephites – A major part of Book of Mormon history centers around two related, but warring, groups of ancient Americans. (also see Lamanites.) One of those groups was called the Nephites after their common ancestor Nephi (see Nephi). The Nephites were the more righteous of the two groups, but were often only kept from falling into wickedness (or pulled back from apostasy or destruction) by the powerful preaching of God's prophets among them.

Offerings, Fast – Latter-day Saints (see Church, The) are expected to fast two meals on the first weekend of each month and contribute the money they would have spent on those meals as a fast offering to help care for the poor and needy. Church members may choose to fast at other times for spiritual reasons. They also make other offerings of money, property and labor on a consistent basis.

Preach My Gospel – A publication of the Church (see Church, The) that serves as a training aid for full-time missionaries and members on how to share the gospel of Jesus Christ.

Priesthood Blessings – Latter-day Saints (see Church, The) believe that those who have been ordained as elders in the priesthood have the power and authority to perform ordinances called blessings and that those blessings are given by inspiration from the Holy Ghost. Blessings may be given to those seeking help, comfort, courage, healing and strength.

Saints – Members of The Church of Jesus of Latter-day Saints are often referred to as simply Saints, especially when referring to each other.

Tithing – Members of the Church (see Church, The) believe in and practice the Law of Tithing. It is defined as paying the Lord $1/10^{th}$ of your increase annually. "Increase" has been interpreted by Church leaders as "income". Many members make other financial offerings to the Church in addition to Tithing (see Offerings, Fast).

Ward – The basic congregational unit of the Church (see Church, The). A ward is designated by a set of geographical boundaries and all members who live within those boundaries are assigned to that ward. Each ward will have around 250 to 500 members depending on their location. Each ward is presided over by a pastor called a bishop (see Bishop) and is organized and administered according to the instructions in Church Handbooks 1 and 2. (see Handbook 2).

Zarahemla – The chief and capital city of the Nephite Nation (see Nephites) in the Book of Mormon (see Book of Mormon).